The Princeton Review
PrincetonReview.com

W9-CIE-837

Cracking the 3rd Grade

Reading & Math

A Parent's Guide to
Helping Your Child
Excel in School

By Lisa Elmore, Diane Milne, Wendy Scheir,
and the Staff of the Princeton Review

Random House, Inc.
New York

RandomHouse.com

The Princeton Review is one of the nation's leaders in test preparation and a pioneer in the world of education. The Princeton Review offers a broad range of products and services to measurably improve academic performance for millions of students every year.

The Princeton Review is not affiliated with Princeton University or Educational Testing Service.

The Princeton Review, Inc.
2315 Broadway
New York, NY 10024
E-mail: booksupport@review.com

Published in the United States by Random House, Inc., New York

ISBN: 978-0-375-76604-6

Printed in the United States of America

9 8 7 6 5 4 3 2 1

First Edition

CREDITS

Series Editor: Casey Cornelius

Content Editor: Sherine Gilmour

Development Editor: Rachael Nevins

Production Editor: Melissa Lewis

Art Director: Neil McMahon

Senior Designer: Doug McGredy

Production Manager: Greta Blau

Production Coordinator: Leif Osgood

Illustrators: Doug McGredy, Tom Racine, and Tim Goldman

ACKNOWLEDGMENTS

This book would not have been possible without the contributions of a talented team of writers, editors, artists, and developers, who tackled this series with devotion and smarts.

CONTENTS

139 MATH

Introduction

You and Your Kid

Your job is to help your child excel in school. Everyone agrees that children bloom when their parents, family, friends, and neighbors nudge them to learn—from the Department of Education to the Parent Teacher Association, from research organizations known as "educational laboratories" to the local newspaper, from the National Endowment for the Arts to kids' shows on TV.

But state standards hardly make for enjoyable leisure reading, and plowing through reports on the best ways to teach math and reading can leave you with a headache, rubbing your temples. You're caught in the middle: you want to help your kid, but it's not always easy to know how.

That's where *Cracking the Third Grade* comes in. We identified the core skills that third graders need to know. Then, we put them together along with some helpful tips for you and fun activities for your kid. We built this book to be user-friendly, so you and your kid can fit in some quality time, even as you're juggling all your other parental responsibilities.

A Parent's Many Hats

As a parent, you're a cook, a chaffeur, a coach, an ally, and oh so many other things. So, keep it simple. Check out these ways you can use *Ahead of the Curve* to get involved in your child's academic life.

Teacher. You taught your kid how to cross the street and tie his or her shoes. In addition, you may have worked to teach your child academic skills by reviewing definitions, helping your child memorize facts, and explaining concepts to your child. By doing so, you are modeling a great learning attitude and great study habits for your child. You are teaching him or her the value of school.

Nurturer. As a nurturer, you're always there to support your child through tough times, celebrate your child's successes, and give your child rules and limits. You encourage your child while holding high expectations. All of this can help your child feel safe and supported enough to face challenges and opportunities at school, such as tests, projects, new teachers, and so on.

Intermediary. You are your child's first representative in the world. You're the main go-between and communicator for your child (school-to-home and home-to-school).

Advocate. As an advocate, you can do many things: sit on advisory councils at school, assist in the classroom, join the PTA, volunteer in school programs, vote in school board elections, and argue for learning standards and approaches you believe in.

· · · · · · · · · · · · ● ● ● ●

Sometimes it's hard to know what to do, and it's easy to feel overwhelmed. But remember, it's not all on your shoulders. Research shows that family and close friends all have a huge effect on kids' academic success.

What's in This Book

The Skill
Each lesson targets a key third-grade skill. You and your kid can either work on all the lessons or pick and choose the lessons you want. If time is short, your kid can work on an activity without reviewing an entire lesson.

Just for You
Tips, advice, insight, and clues from parents and educators start here! Read this before diving into the rest of the lesson.

First Things First
This is the starting point for your kid in every lesson.

Supplies
Get your kid in the habit of gathering supplies before starting a lesson.

Jump Right In!
These are questions for your kid to complete independently. Give your kid as much time as he or she needs. But if your kid takes more than 30 minutes, consider the possibility that he or she may be having a hard time focusing, be unfamiliar with the skill, or have difficulty with the skill.

Range, Mode, and Mean

We live in a data-driven world filled with information about everything from how many people live in a certain area to who likes what flavor ice cream. We use data to make key decisions: what doctor to choose, what dinner to eat, how much to pay for things, and so on. While data is crucial, sometimes it seems our lives are dominated by data. We wonder what our kids' futures will be—strapping techno-gadgets to their brains, crunching numbers all the time, following streams of flowing data?

You know that your kids need to be comfortable understanding and using data. It's key for their lives today, and it's absolutely crucial for the future that they will be a part of creating.

By thinking about data in terms of range, mode, and mean, your child is starting to practice "viewing" data as a resource. The numbers aren't something to be memorized (there are too many numbers and sets of data in the world to memorize them all!)—the numbers are something to be understood. By having a chance to play around with range, mode, and mean, your kid can get more comfortable looking at data, pondering it, analyzing it, and even developing opinions about it.

First things first: Get a sense of what your kid already knows. Turn the page and tell your kid to Jump Right In!

Here's what you'll need for this lesson:
- paper
- pencils
- timer or clock

Jump Right In!

1. $3 \times 4 =$
  A. 1
  B. 7
  C. 9

3. $6 \times 0 =$
  A. 0
  B. 5

Checking In ....
Check your kid's answers to the Jump Right In! questions. Whether your kid aced the Jump Right In! questions or had some trouble, here's stuff you can do to keep supporting your kid.

 Checking In

ⓐAnswers for page 13:

1. A

2. C

3. An A+ answer: "Primates are animals such as apes, gorillas, and mo
The story says that these animals are examples of primates and tha
their hands and feet to hold on to things."

4. An A+ answer: "Aquatic means something that lives in the water. T
says that fish and turtles are aquatic animals that live in the water

Did your child get the correct answers? If so, ask your child to point out the
clues in the story that showed the meaning of the words *watch* and *sign*.

Did your child get one of the answers wrong? If so, explain to your child that
watch and *sign* have more than one meaning. Review the answer choices to q
and 2 and talk about the various meanings of the words *watch* and *sign*.

Watch Out! ....
These tips identify common pitfalls and help you help your child avoid them.

 Watch Out!

Sometimes third graders try to figure out a word's meaning by using the det
find the most interesting. For example, did your child select the wrong mea
word "watch" in question 1? Maybe he or she was thinking about watchi

What to Know... ......
Review these key skills, definitions, and examples with your kid. Questions and tips are provided so you and your kid can talk about the skills.

What to Know . . .

Kids use division all the time when they are sharing. Review these skills wit
child this way.

- **Equal groups** are groups that have the same number of items in th

- **Division** is an operation on two numbers that tells how many grou
  It also tells how many items are in each group. The **division sign**

- The **quotient** is a number resulting from dividing a number by ano
  number. For example, in 24 ÷ 8 = 3, the quotient is 3.

Third Graders Are... ....
Your child's natural stages of growth can play into academic success. These tips give you insider info on the developmental stages of your child and how to help your child through his or her transitions.

Third-Graders Are

Most third graders are just no
hitting the developmental pe
when they can really begin to
think abstractly. Division is a
abstract concept. Some third

On Your Way to an 'A'
Fun, educational activities your kid can do with you, family, neighbors, babysitters, and friends at home, in the car, during errands—anywhere.

On Your Way to an "A" Activities

{ **15** minutes }

Type: Art
Materials needed: Paper, scissors, a
Number of players: 2 or more

Play "Starry, starry night." Fold a piece of paper in ha
out half of a star that includes part of the fold. When
up the paper, you'll have a whole symmetrical star. T
this time, fold the paper twice. Cut out part of a star
both folds. Try making stars with many folds. Then h
around your room!

Study Right
Who hasn't heard that study skills can make or break a student? Check out these tips for study skills your kid can apply immediately.

 Study Right

Conducting research can help your child learn. Research symmetry
Use a folder with two pockets. Label the left pocket "Asymmetrical"
pocket "Symmetrical." Collect pictures as examples of asymmetrical
shapes. Work with your child to identify the shapes and to put them
pocket. Go through the pictures with your child and discuss why one
symmetry while another does not.

*Has your child breezed through the activities? If so, he or she can wor
Your Head activity independently.*

Using Your Head

{ **10** minutes }

*Grab a **pencil** and some **crayons** or **markers**!*

Read each problem. Decide if you have to add or su
the word "add" or "subtract" to show what you nee
Then, solve the problem.

Using Your Head
If your kid feels confident, here's an independent, challenging activity where your kid can show off what he or she knows.

How Does Your Kid Learn Best?

Did you know that your kid learns in a lot of different ways? When kids learn, they use their minds, their bodies, and their senses—sight, sound, taste, touch, and smell.

Some kids can succceed in any classroom, while others need specialized learning support, but all of them have strengths and weaknesses. Your kid can learn to rely on his or her strengths and then work on any weaknesses. This book is full of activities that address each of these learning styles.

Visually—Using Our Sense of Sight
Your kid may learn best by looking at pictures, outlines, maps, and such. Your kid may like to draw pictures or take notes.

Auditory—Using Our Sense of Sound
Your kid may learn best by listening to teachers speak, discussing with friends and classmates, and listening to music while studying. Your kid may like to tap a rhythm with his or her pen or pencil while studying.

Kinesthetic—Using Our Sense of Touch and Movement
Your kid may learn best by moving, taking action, or walking around.

How to Use Learning Styles

Talk with your child about his or her successes at school, home, or with hobbies. How did your child learn what he or she needed to succeed? Knowing how your child learns best can help you make the most of your child's natural strengths and work on your child's weaknesses.

Once you know how your child likes to learn, you can make sure your child includes those learning methods that work (especially when studying for important tests). You can also support your child as he or she tries out more challenging learning methods. In the long run, this will help your child become a well-rounded learner!

 *The Goal*

You know getting involved with your child's school experiences is the right decision. But here's a reminder of some of the rewards you may reap!

Research shows that getting involved in your kid's school experiences can result in:

- Increased academic performance

- Better behavior at school

- Increased academic motivation

- Better school attendance

And lest you think your kid reaps all the rewards, you might find that helping your child learn gives you:

- More info about your kid's school

- A greater sense of your own learning preferences

- More appreciation for all the work you did as a student

- A better relationship with your child's teacher and school staff

Want to Know More?

Check out these Web sites and organizations for more reading and math support.

Family Math and Matemática Para La Familia. If you want information about more effectively helping your child in mathematics, go to http://equals.lhs.berkeley.edu/.

MAPPS (Math and Parent Partnerships). If you want activities and mini-courses to learn about becoming more engaged in your child's school mathematics program, go to http://math.arizona.edu/~mapps/.

National Parent School Partnership (PSP) Program. If you want to better understand parental rights, the structure of schools, and how to enhance parent/teacher conferences, go to www.maldef.org/psp.

Parent Information and Resource Centers (PIRCs). If you want information about your rights under the No Child Left Behind Act as well as training, advocates, or other assistance, go to www.ed.gov/programs/pirc/index.html.

Parents for Public Schools. If you want to find out about chapters of parents working together to advocate for school improvement, go to www.parents4publicschools.com.

PTA (Parent Teacher Association). If you want to connect with other parents involved in local schools, go to www.pta.org.

Parent Training and Information Centers. If you want to find out about education and services to assist a child with disabilities, go to www.taalliance.org/centers/index.htm.

PESA (Parent Expectations Support Achievement). If you want techniques for improving your child's academic achievement, go to http://streamer.lacoe.edu/pesa/.

PIQE (Parent Institute for Quality Education). If you want to learn about how to motivate your child in school, develop a home learning environment, work with the school system, or prepare for college, go to www.pique.org.

Reading Is Fundamental. If you want help with supporting your child's reading and learning, go to www.rif.org.

Reading

Using Context

You've helped your kid learn to read. You've worked hard to help your child read independently. When your child didn't know a word, you might have said, "Look it up in a dictionary" or "Look at the pictures to figure out what the word means."

But sometimes there isn't a dictionary around. And as your child learns to read more challenging books, there won't be as many pictures that can tip off your kid to the meaning of unfamiliar words.

Most of the time, your kid probably guesses at the meaning of words she doesn't know. But when your child is "guessing," she may actually be using context clues. You can help her learn to use context clues actively to make reading a richer and more rewarding experience.

First things first: Get a sense of what your kid already knows. Turn the page and tell your kid to Jump Right In!

Here's what you'll need for this lesson:
- *comic books or comic strips*
- *paper*
- *pencil*
- *crayons or markers*
- *movies*
- *dictionary*

 **Jump Right In!**

What's Happening at the Zoo?

Carla and her family went to the zoo. They were meeting the rest of their family there. When they got to the zoo, Carla saw her aunts, uncles, and cousins. Her cousin Ella waved to her.

Everyone was excited to spend the day together. They needed to decide what animals to see first. Carla saw a <u>sign</u> that showed a map of the zoo.

Then, Ella grabbed a list of the showtimes. The lion feeding was at 11:00 a.m. Carla's dad checked his <u>watch</u>. They had an hour before the show began.

"I'd like to see the apes, gorillas, and monkeys, so let's see the <u>primates</u> first," Ella said. "I love how they use their hands and feet to hold on to things."

"Great!" said Carla. "After that, let's see the <u>aquatic</u> animals. I like to look through the glass and watch the fish swim through the water. I also like watching the turtles spin around in the water. They're great swimmers."

Carla's dad smiled. "You girls have the day planned out already."

"We don't want to miss a thing!" said Carla.

"Yeah, let's get started," Ella said. "We have a lot to see today!"

1. Find the word *watch* in the story. In which sentence below does *watch* have the same meaning as in the story?

   A. He wore a watch on his right arm.

   B. Will you watch me dance?

   C. She likes to watch baseball.

   D. They kept watch over the campfire.

2. Find the word *sign* in the story. In which sentence below does *sign* have the same meaning as in the story?

   A. Mom has to sign the check to pay for groceries.

   B. Clouds are a sign that it may rain.

   C. The sign says the store opens at 9:00 a.m.

   D. Will you please sign my paper?

3. What does the word *primate* mean in the story?

   _____

   _____

4. What does the word *aquatic* mean in the story?

   _____

   _____

   _____

Excellent Job!

 *Checking In*

ⒶAnswers for page 13:

    1. A

    2. C

    3. An A+ answer: "Primates are animals such as apes, gorillas, and monkeys. The story says that these animals are examples of primates and that they use their hands and feet to hold onto things."

    4. An A+ answer: "*Aquatic* means something that lives in the water. The story says that fish and turtles are aquatic animals that live in the water."

Did your child get the correct answers? If so, ask your child to point out the context clues in the story that showed the meaning of the words *watch* and *sign*.

Did your child get any of the answers wrong? If so, explain to your child that the words *watch* and *sign* have more than one meaning. Review the answer choices to questions 1 and 2 and talk about the various meanings of the words *watch* and *sign*. Talk about how to determine the meanings of these words in their given sentences. Then, ask your child to find these words in the passage and identify what these words mean in that context. Ask your child to try to answer questions 1 and 2 again.

 *Watch Out!*

Sometimes third graders try to figure out a word's meaning by using the details they find the most interesting. For example, did your child select the wrong meaning for the word *watch* in question 1? Maybe he or she was thinking about watching animals at the zoo, rather than using the context clues like "11:00 a.m." and "an hour." Help your child get in the habit of pointing out clues.

What to Know...

Your kid uses context clues all the time: to play video games, to figure out unknown words, to solve puzzles, and in other everyday activities.

Review these skills with your child this way:

- **Context clues** are words and phrases around an unknown word in a passage that help you figure out the meaning of the unknown word.

- **Multiple-meaning words** are words that have several different meanings depending on how they are used in the sentence.

You and your child might read this sign at a zoo.

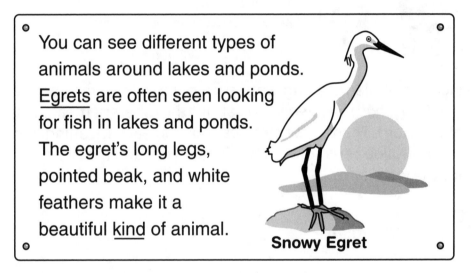

You can see different types of animals around lakes and ponds. <u>Egrets</u> are often seen looking for fish in lakes and ponds. The egret's long legs, pointed beak, and white feathers make it a beautiful <u>kind</u> of animal.

Snowy Egret

Ask your child to use context clues to figure out what an *egret* is.

Here are some context clues that can help your child figure out that an *egret* is a bird:

- long legs
- pointed beak
- white feathers

Tell your child that *kind* can mean *type* or *nice*. Ask your child to use context clues to tell the meaning of the word *kind* in the zoo sign.

On Your Way to an "A" Activities

5 minutes

Type: Active
Materials needed: comic books or comic strips
Number of players: 2 or more

Choose a comic. Find a word you know. Then, look for clues in the comic that could help someone else learn the meaning of the word. Take turns. Then, find a word in the comic you do not know. Look for clues to help you find the meaning.

10 minutes

Type: Arts and Crafts
Materials needed: paper and markers or crayons
Number of players: 2 or more

Pick a multiple-meaning word such as *race, bank, face, pen, bowl, ring, bat, sink,* or *pet*. Talk about the different meanings of the word. Then, draw pictures showing each meaning. For example, you could draw a black bat flying and a baseball bat for the word *bat*.

 Study Right

Make a personal dictionary with your child. Whenever your child finds words he or she doesn't know, add these words and their definitions to the dictionary. Ask your child to draw pictures in the dictionary showing the meaning of the new words. Encourage your child to use the new words in writing and in conversation when possible. Explain that building vocabulary helps people to become better readers and writers.

5 minutes

Type: Speaking/Listening
Materials needed: none
Number of players: 2 or more

Make up a new word. Think of a meaning for your word. Use your word in a sentence that includes context clues that tell the word's meaning. For example, "I like taking *snarfdow* lessons. I practice the instrument every day and am able to play beautiful songs." Say this sentence aloud. The other players need to use the context clues to figure out the meaning of your made-up word. Take turns making up zany words and coming up with clues.

10 minutes

Type: Game/Competitive
Materials needed: movies, dictionary, paper, pencil
Number of players: 2 or more

Watch a movie. Whenever you hear a word you don't know, try to figure out its meaning based on clues in the movie. Write the word and then write a list of clues on a piece of paper. The other players should identify different unknown words and write them with clues on a piece of paper. Pause the movie. Then, talk with the other players about the words to figure out their meaning. Check your work by looking up the words in a dictionary. If you can't find them in a dictionary, ask your parent to review how you spelled your word. Keep playing as you watch the movie.

 *Checking In*

Your kid may pick out details that are not context clues. Ask your child to draw a picture for each unknown word he identifies in the movie from the last activity. Then, tell your child to label what he drew and use his labeled drawing to figure out the meaning of the unknown word.

Has your child breezed through the activities? If so, he or she can work on this Using Your Head activity independently.

Using Your Head

[10 minutes]

*Grab some **crayons** or **markers**!*

Look at the picture. Read the words in the word bank. For each word, choose the meaning that is shown in the picture. Color the picture to show the correct meaning.

Sink: to go underwater—Red

Sink: something that holds water—Blue

Can: to know how—Orange

Can: a metal container—Yellow

Bowl: a round dish—Green

Bowl: to roll a ball in bowling—Purple

Pet: a household animal—Brown

Pet: to rub or pat—Black

Answers: Sink—blue; Can—yellow; Bowl—green; Pet (dog)—brown

Before Reading

Your child might rush headlong into every new activity. Why slow down and think? Just jump headfirst into everything! Ah, the excitement of being young! But there are times when a little preparation can really pay off. Reading is one of those times.

Kids need to set a purpose for reading before opening a book. Your kid needs to know if she is reading for enjoyment or if she is supposed to be looking for information. She needs to warm up to what she is going to read in order to get the most out of it. She also needs to think about what she already knows about the topic, and think about what she might learn through reading.

First things first: Get a sense of what your kid already knows. Turn the page and tell your kid to Jump Right In!

Here's what you'll need for this lesson:
- *magazine photos*
- *pencils*
- *index cards*
- *tape*
- *movie or TV show on tape*
- *timer*

 **Jump Right In!**

Everyone Loves a Parade!

Jamal could hardly wait. His dad said they were going to spend the day together doing something special, but he had not said what they would do. In the car, Jamal was so curious that he had to ask, "What are we going to do?"

"Well," his dad said, "I'll give you hints. We are going to see clowns."

"Are we going to the circus?" Jamal asked.

"No," said his dad. "We will also see marching bands."

"Are we going to a football game?" Jamal asked.

"No," said his dad. "We will also see floats in the street."

"Now I know!" Jamal said. "We're going to a parade!"

Soon, they got out of the car. Jamal and his dad walked hand in hand through the crowd. The first band marched toward them. Jamal could hear the drums. He could feel the beating in his chest. After that, clowns ran down the street. Some threw beads. Some threw candy. Jamal got to shake hands with one of the clowns.

Behind the clowns was the first float. It had a lot of bright colors. People on the float waved. Jamal waved back. Then, he looked up at his dad. "Thanks, Dad! This is the best parade ever!"

1. Why might you read a story about a parade?

    A. to enjoy the story

    B. to learn about floats

    C. to get ready for a test

    D. to learn how to be a clown

2. Read the end of the story. What do you think happened next?

    A. The parade stopped.

    B. People played football.

    C. The first float passed by.

    D. Elephants marched past.

3. The title of the story is "Everyone Loves a Parade!" What does this title make you think about?

    _____

    _____

4. What would you expect to see at a parade?

    _____

    _____

Excellent Job!

 *Checking In*

Answers for page 21:

    1. A

    2. C

    3. An A+ answer: "I think about people who are excited to see a parade. I think about all the fun stuff to see at a parade."

    4. An A+ answer: "I know parades sometimes have funny cars, dancers, and large balloons in different shapes. I also know that usually a lot of people go to parades."

Did your child get the correct answers? If so, ask your child to draw a picture of what he thought about when he read the story.

Did your child get any of the answers wrong? If so, ask your child to talk through how she picked the answer. Ask, "What answer choices do you think are wrong and why?" and "Is that answer based on the information in the passage?"

 *Watch Out!*

Sometimes third graders have trouble making predictions based on the text. They may make predictions based on what they would like to see happen. For example, with question 2, it might be a lot of fun to see elephants pass by. But the passage did not mention elephants. Review each answer choice with your child, and ask your child to point out any details in the passage that support each choice. Then, ask your child to identify the answer choice that is best supported by the passage.

What to Know...

Your kid gets warmed up to play a game: learns the rules, stretches, gets supplies, or remembers previous games. But your kid may not know how to get warmed up to read.

Review these skills with your child this way:

- **Prior knowledge** is any relevant information we have before we begin reading.

- A **prediction** is an idea or thought about the future.

- Strong readers set a **purpose** for reading—they know if they are reading to get information or to have fun. To get information, people might read newspapers, instruction manuals, editorials, essays, dictionaries, cookbooks, and other texts. To have fun, people might read poems, novels, plays, short stories, and other texts.

Remembering prior knowledge can help your kid understand what he or she is reading. Your kid might remember:

- Sports can be played outside and inside.

- There are different kinds of sports, like baseball, basketball, swimming, kickball, and others.

Strong readers know that they can read for a lot of reasons. Make sure your kid predicts that "How to Win at Every Sport" tells information about how to play sports better. So, your kid would read it to get information. "How I Beat Aliens at Basketball" probably has made-up stories that your kid could read for fun.

On Your Way to an "A" Activities

 5 minutes

Type: Speaking/Listening
Materials needed: magazine photos
Number of players: 2 or more

Choose a picture in a magazine. Talk about what it reminds you of. Maybe you have done the same thing as the people in the picture. Maybe you have been to the same place. With the other players, talk about what is happening. Decide what you think will probably happen next.

  5 minutes

Type: Active
Materials needed: pencils, 30 index cards, tape
Number of players: you

Write "For Fun" on 15 index cards. Write "To Learn" on 15 index cards. Walk around your house. When you find something you read for fun, tape a "For Fun" index card on it. When you find something you read so you can learn, tape a "To Learn" index card on it. Then, notice if you have anything you read for fun *and* in order to learn!

Type: Game/Competitive
Materials needed: a movie or TV show on tape
Number of players: 2 or more

Play a movie or TV show. After watching for a little while, press "Pause." With the other players, predict what might happen next. Then, press "Play" and see if your prediction is right. Take turns pressing "Pause" and making predictions. Each time one of your predictions is correct, you earn a point. See who has made the most correct predictions by the end of the movie or show. That player is the winner!

Type: Game/Competitive
Materials needed: index cards, pencil, a timer
Number of players: 2 or more

Share the index cards with the other players. Write a different topic on each card (like ice cream, Saturdays, sports, outer space, and others). Shuffle the index cards together, and then pick one card. Read the topic aloud. Then, ask the other players to list everything they know about the topic in one minute. Use the timer. Give each player one point for each item he or she listed. Take turns. Whoever has the most points wins the round. Continue by playing another round!

Has your child breezed through the activities? If so, he or she can work on this Using Your Head activity independently.

Using Your Head

{**10** minutes}

Grab a **pencil**!

Look at the book covers. Circle two books you would read for fun. Draw a square around two books you would read to learn information.

To learn: *How to Play the Trombone* and *Tips for Playing the Tuba*
Answers: For fun: *Tootie Trumpet's Trip to Town* and *Freddy the Frog Finds a Flute*;

During Reading: Connections

Have you ever heard your kid say, "I love that movie. The main character was just like me!" or "I have to get this toy. It's part of the series!" Have you ever stood astonished as your child listed a series of precise details about how some new video game was based on some older video game? If so, then your kid is making connections.

Making connections is how we make sense of the world around us, but it's another skill that your kid might have trouble applying in school. Worried about the "right" answer or doubtful in unfamiliar territory, your kid might make connections that are tentative or vague. Even if your kid is comfortable with making connections, strengthening this skill can still benefit your child. Help your kid by reinforcing that he has valuable ideas and by showing him how to connect those ideas to the things he reads in school.

First things first: Get a sense of what your kid already knows. Turn the page and tell your kid to Jump Right In!

Here's what you'll need for this lesson:
- empty shopping bags
- books
- newspapers
- pencils

 **Jump Right In!**

Amy's Airplane Adventure

Amy missed her Aunt Debbie. Last summer, her aunt had moved to the other side of the country. They wrote letters, sent e-mails, and talked on the phone, but Amy had not seen her favorite aunt in nearly a year.

Then, Amy read a very exciting e-mail from Aunt Debbie. "I can't wait to see you in a few weeks," she read.

"Mom!" Amy yelled. "Aunt Debbie is coming to visit!"

"No," her mom said. "She is not coming here. You are going to go see her!"

Amy was thrilled. She jumped up and down. But then she stopped.

"Mom," Amy asked, "how will I get there?"

"You are going to fly on a plane by yourself," her mom said.

Amy felt a knot in her stomach and a lump in her throat. Tears began to burn her eyes. She had never flown on a plane alone.

Her mom could see she was upset. So, they went to the library. They got books about airplanes. They read stories about flying. They went to the airport and looked around. They watched the planes take off and land. They even got to talk to a pilot.

Soon, Amy was excited about her trip. She could not wait to see Aunt Debbie, and she could not wait to fly!

1. At the beginning of the story, Amy was reading and writing e-mails. Who else reads and writes e-mails in this story?

A. Aunt Debbie

B. Amy's mom

C. the pilot

D. the librarian

2. At first, Amy was upset about flying. How did she feel about flying by the end of the story?

A. She was still afraid.

B. She did not want to go.

C. She was sad.

D. She was excited.

3. How would you feel about flying alone? Explain.

_____

_____

_____

4. In the story, Amy can e-mail her aunt. E-mail was just invented in the last century. How do you think people used to communicate with each other before e-mail? Did Amy use any of these ways?

_____

_____

_____

Excellent Job!

Checking In

A Answers for page 29:

1. A

2. D

3. An A+ answer: "I would be afraid of flying alone because I would not know anyone. I've never been that far away from my family, and going on a trip by myself would be scary at first. Once I got there, it would be fun."

4. An A+ answer: "Before e-mail, people used the phone and regular mail to communicate. The story said Amy also talked to her aunt on the phone, and they sent letters to each other."

Did your child get the correct answers? If so, have your child show you where in the story he or she found the answer.

Did your child get any of the answers wrong? If so, ask, "Why did you choose that answer?" Maybe your child thought about his or her own experiences, rather than Amy's experiences in the story. For example, for question 2, maybe your child thought about how he or she would feel about flying, rather than how Amy felt. You could say, "Let's read that part of the story again. Tell me when you hear the answer to question 2."

Watch Out!

In third grade, kids are becoming more aware of the world around them. If a certain issue is on your child's mind, he or she may try to relate that issue to a story, even if there are no details in the text to support this. Think about what your child sees on the news or is learning about our world. Hurricanes, airport security, poverty, professional sports play-offs, and upcoming local events may be the big stories on the evening news each night. Your child may think Amy is sad about flying because she'll miss the opening of the new museum downtown, if that is something your family has been looking forward to. Help keep your kid on track by pointing out that connections should be related to what's happening in the story.

What to Know...

Your child makes connections in all sorts of situations.

Review these skills with your child this way:

- **Text-to-text connections** are when you build links and relationships between different parts of a text. For example, you can build links between texts, such as from a story to a poem, story, movie, or song. You can also link details from the beginning of a text to the end of a text.

- **Text-to-self connections** are when you make links and relationships between the text and your everyday life, personal experiences, and private thoughts or feelings.

- **Text-to-world connections** are when you build links and relationships between the text and the world. You can link details from the text with the things you see in the world and events going on in the world.

Imagine that you and your child see someone at the store purchasing luggage.

Ask your child to look at the picture. Ask your child to connect the picture with anything in the story "Amy's Airplane Adventure." Then, ask if anything he or she experienced in life comes to mind. Finally, ask if anything about the world comes to mind.

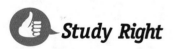 **Study Right**

Making word webs can help your child see connections and organize ideas. Draw a circle in the center of a piece of paper. In it, write "Amy's Airplane Adventure." Then, draw three circles around it and label them "Text-to-Text" (the picture of a person buying luggage), "Text-to-Self," and "Text-to-World," respectively. Draw a line to connect each of these circles with the center circle. Each time you or your child makes a connection, decide what type of connection it is. Then, write the connection next to the circle for that type of connection.

Here are some examples of **text-to-text** connections:

- "Amy will need to pack a suitcase to visit her aunt. This person might pack the suitcase to visit someone."
- "Amy's aunt probably needed to use suitcases when she moved. This person might use the suitcase in a move."

If your child is unsure how to make a text-to-text connection, ask, "Can you imagine Amy in the picture? If so, what is she doing?" Encourage your child to draw Amy into the picture.

Here are some examples of **text-to-self** connections:

- "We packed suitcases before visiting Grandma. This person might pack the suitcase to visit someone."
- "We store our winter clothes in suitcases, so maybe the person in the picture will store things in the suitcase."

Are your child's text-to-self connections vague? If so, ask your child to point out a detail in the picture and explain how he or she shares or relates to that detail or is different from that detail.

Here are some examples of **text-to-world** connections:

- "Our neighbor has to travel for work and uses suitcases. I wonder if this person is traveling for work."
- "I see teachers and students using small suitcases to carry books and supplies. I wonder if this person has to carry supplies for a job."

If your child is having trouble making links between the picture and the world, he or she may be overwhelmed by the word *world*. Remind your child of familiar things in the world. For example, about travel, you could remind your child of suitcases in the home; visits by car, bus, train, or airplane; and scenes of travel on TV.

On Your Way to an "A" Activities

{ 10 minutes }
Type: Active
Materials needed: empty shopping bags
Number of players: 2 or more

With the other players, pick a favorite story, song, movie, or TV show. Then, go on a scavenger hunt. Find things that remind you of some part of your favorite story. Collect several things. Then, share your items with the other players. Tell why each reminds you of the story.

{ 10 minutes }
Type: Game/Competitive
Materials needed: books and newspaper
Number of players: 2 or more

Choose a book with the other players. Read the first page. Then, look in the newspaper for something that is connected to what you've read in the story. Take turns reading and looking for connections in the newspaper. Whenever a player makes a connection, he or she gets one point.

Third Graders Are...

Third graders are full of energy. After sitting all day in school, your child may not be thrilled with sitting to do anything else. But who says you have to sit still to do these activities? Let your child stand up or sit on a swing to read. Or lay on the floor together. Learning does not have to happen at the kitchen table.

Has your child breezed through the activities? If so, he or she can work on this Using Your Head activity independently.

Using Your Head

[10 minutes]

Grab a pencil!

Amy is reading about airplanes. She has made five connections. Draw a line from each of her connections to the correct category.

1. People fly around the world.
2. I will fly to see my aunt.
3. Both books show pictures of airplanes.
4. There are airports in different countries.
5. I like these books.

Answers: Text-to-Text—3; Text-to-Self—2 and 5; Text-to-World—1 and 4

During Reading: Checking Understanding

Imagine that your child is reading aloud to you. At the end of the book, you realize that he or she has not missed a single word! Every word was pronounced correctly. Your child stopped at every period. Has the challenge of reading been conquered? Not necessarily. Just because your kid can read something does not mean that he or she understands the book.

Kids can get so wrapped up in sounding out words that they forget to pay attention to the meaning of the story. They can make it through an entire book and have only a vague idea of what they have just read. Your child might not realize that being confused about what he reads is completely normal. It's all part of learning how to become a strong reader. As a parent, you want to encourage your kid to understand that confusion is natural. You also want to give your kid easy, helpful ways of dealing with confusion. Once your kid knows how to deal with confusion, he can really dig into his favorite books.

First things first: Get a sense of what your kid already knows. Turn the page and tell your kid to Jump Right In!

Here's what you'll need for this lesson:
- *magazines*
- *paper*
- *crayons or markers*
- *pencils*

Jump Right In!

Tyrone's Sunny Saturday

I feel the sun shine on my face
and the sand between my toes.
I listen to the crashing ocean waves
and smell salt air in my nose.

We spread the blanket on the perfect spot,
and I take the shovel in my hand.
I start to dig and begin to build
a castle made from sand.

I look for shells and bring them back
to make castle windows and doors.
Then my sister and I take a swim
and ride the waves back to shore.

We take a break for our picnic lunch,
then find shells to take back home.
We swim and play until the day grows cool,
and then it's time to go.

1. Tyrone found seashells. What quote describes what he did with the seashells?

   A. "to dig and begin to build a castle"

   B. "to make castle windows and doors"

   C. to "play until the day grows cool"

   D. to "listen to the crashing ocean waves"

2. Which of these questions is <u>not</u> answered by the poem?

   A. What does Tyrone feel between his toes?

   B. What does Tyrone build with sand?

   C. What does Tyrone smell?

   D. What did Tyrone eat for lunch?

3. Imagine "Tyrone's Sunny Saturday." Draw what you imagine here.

4. What questions do you have about Tyrone?

   _____

   _____

   _____

   _____

Excellent Job!

Checking In

Answers for page 37:

1. B

2. D

3. An A+ answer: Your child should draw a picture of Tyrone at the beach. Your child could include details such as a sand castle with seashell doors and windows, a picnic lunch, waves, and Tyrone's sister.

4. An A+ answer: Your child should write questions about the poem, such as "Why did Tyrone go the beach?"; "How many shells did they find?"; and so on.

Did your child get the correct answers? If so, ask your child to come up with one question about each of the stanzas in the poem.

Did your child get any of the answers wrong? If so, ask, "Did you check your answer by going back to the poem?" Maybe your child didn't think to make sure that his answer is supported by details in the poem. Review the answer choices and ask your child to locate details in the poem that show whether the answer choice is correct or incorrect.

Third Graders Are...

Third graders are not always ready to admit when they are confused or when something is hard. Instead, they may say things like "This is boring" or "Why do I have to do this?" Find out if your kid is frustrated or insecure, and explain that confusion is a natural part of the reading process. The strongest readers get confused. Also, find out how to help your child through his or her confusion. Maybe your kid might find it more satisfying to read if he or she read a different book or if you read together.

What to Know...

Your kid may not know when he misunderstood something he read. Or he might know he is confused but not know how to fix it.

Review these skills with your child in this way:

- **Picture the story.** Strong readers develop their comprehension by picturing the story (imagining the details and the actions) as they read.

- **Check understanding and clear up confusion.** Strong readers check their understanding. They ask themselves questions before they read, while they read, and after they read. When strong readers identify that they are confused, they take the time to answer their questions before they continue reading, and they use details from the story whenever possible.

Your kid might read instructions for an arts and crafts project.

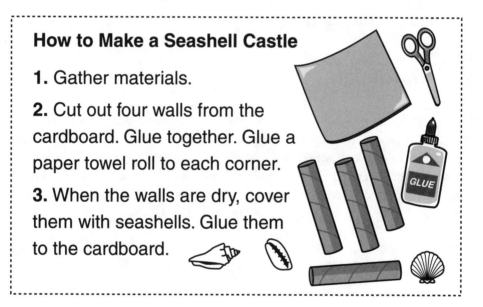

How to Make a Seashell Castle

1. Gather materials.

2. Cut out four walls from the cardboard. Glue together. Glue a paper towel roll to each corner.

3. When the walls are dry, cover them with seashells. Glue them to the cardboard.

Ask your child to think of at least one question just by looking at the pictures and the steps. Talk about possible answers. Then, ask your child to think of a question after each step and talk about possible answers.

Your kid might come up with questions about the details in the story. Maybe your kid understood most of the castle directions but missed some details.

- Should I wait for the walls to dry before I glue on the seashells?

- What materials will I need?

Can your kid find the details in the castle directions or artwork to answer his or her questions?

Sometimes kids have questions about what they feel or think about a story. Your kid might wonder:

- How does that make me feel?

- Am I supposed to feel what the character feels, or can I feel something different?

- What do I want to happen?

 ## Watch Out!

Children struggling with reading comprehension can come up with some pretty far-fetched questions, unrelated to what they read. They can also draw a blank when asked if they have any questions. For example, your child might ask, "Did Tyrone have glue at the beach?" Or did your child not understand the story but not have any questions? If so, model asking questions when you read books, newspapers, street signs, anything! Show your child it's okay to be confused.

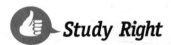 ## Study Right

A picture can say a thousand words. But drawing pictures can also help your kid keep track of what she is reading. Ask her to further develop her picture of the poem about Tyrone or to illustrate the directions for building the seashell castle. Then, have her label the picture. Check that the picture shows the details correctly. Your kid can peek at the pictures whenever she needs a quick way to check her understanding.

On Your Way to an "A" Activities

10 minutes

Type: Speaking/Listening
Materials needed: magazines
Number of players: 2 or more

Choose a picture from a magazine. With the other players, talk about what is happening in the picture. Then, think of questions you have about the picture. List several questions. Then, tell a story about the picture. Be sure to answer all of your questions in your story.

10 minutes

Type: Arts and Crafts
Materials needed: paper and crayons or markers
Number of players: 2 or more

Draw a picture. Do not let the other players see it. Then, tell them about what you drew. The other players will think about your picture in their minds. Then, the other players will each draw what you described. Compare pictures. See if the other players' pictures look like what you drew. Take turns drawing and describing pictures.

Has your child breezed through the activities? If so, he or she can work on this Using Your Head activity independently.

Using Your Head

{10} minutes

*Grab a **pencil** and some **crayons** or **markers**!*

Picture the poem "Tyrone's Sunny Saturday." Find the things in the picture below that do not make sense based on the details in the poem. Cross them out, then color the rest of the picture.

Answers: The castle door should be a seashell, not a fork. The birthday cake, balloons, birthday hat, and kitten should not be there. Tyrone should have a shovel, not a pail, in his hand.

After Reading

Have you ever asked your child about his or her day, only to end up hearing a minute-by-minute play by play? Often, kids think the more information, the better.

The same thing can happen when your child tells you about a book or story. Your child has worked hard for many years learning to decode words and understand the meaning of what he reads. Now, he wants to show you all the good work he's done by telling you all about his favorite story! While it can be great to get all the details, there are definitely days when you have time to hear only the highlights.

Third graders might not realize how giving a summary can be more effective than telling everything. They might not think about how often they encounter and rely on summaries every day. When picking out a movie, they read summaries of movies. When deciding on what to eat at the cafeteria, they read summaries about what's for lunch (soup with noodles and tomatoes or soup with beef and peas).

Your child uses details and summaries to make choices every day. So, encourage your child to practice summarizing his or her stories.

First things first: Get a sense of what your kid already knows. Turn the page and tell your kid to Jump Right In!

Here's what you'll need for this lesson:
- *paper*
- *index cards*
- *pencils*
- *art supplies such as construction paper, glitter, and glue*
- *crayons or markers*

Jump Right In!

Caring for Hermit Crabs

Hermit crabs make great pets. They are easy to care for and do not need many things. They are also a lot of fun to watch!

Supplies

Your hermit crab will need an old fish tank for a home. He will also need gravel and extra shells. You will need to get small bowls to hold food and water. Be sure the bowls are small! Your hermit crab will need to climb into them—and then be able to climb out of them!

Care

Be sure to keep his home clean. Once a month, empty the fish tank. Rinse everything, but do not use soap. When everything is dry, put your crab back in the tank.

Also, be sure to give your hermit crab food and water every day. You can buy food for him at the pet store. He will also like to eat fresh fruit and vegetables. Your hermit crab will not just need water to drink. He will also need you to sprinkle warm water on him. This will keep him from drying out.

Shells

Hermit crabs have hard shells. They use their shells as homes and as protection. In fact, they rarely leave their shells. Sometimes, though, your hermit crab will grow too big for his shell. He will need a bigger shell. Be sure to keep larger shells in your hermit crab's tank. That way, when the time is right, your hermit crab will choose a new shell home to carry on his back.

1. Which of these is the best summary of the "Supplies" section?

   A. Hermit crabs live in old fish tanks.

   B. You will need a fish tank, gravel, shells, and food bowls to care for a hermit crab.

   C. Hermit crabs crawl in and out of their food and water bowls, so the bowls need to be small.

   D. You need to buy two small bowls so that you can have one bowl for food and one for water.

2. Which of these is a detail from the story?

   A. Hermit crabs are cheap to buy.

   B. Hermit crabs are better pets than cats.

   C. Hermit crabs use shells as protection.

   D. Hermit crabs are hard to care for.

3. Write as many details as you can remember from the passage.

   _____

   _____

   _____

   _____

4. Now, pick the most important details from your list and use them to write a summary of the passage.

   _____

   _____

   _____

Excellent Job!

Checking In

Ⓐ Answers for page 45:

1. B

2. C

3. An A+ answer: "Hermit crabs make great pets and are easy to care for. To have one, you need a fish tank, gravel, and extra shells. You need two small bowls. The bowls should be small because the hermit crab will crawl in and out of them. Be sure to clean the tank once a month, and give the crab food and water every day. Hermit crabs eat food from pet stores and fresh fruit and vegetables. Sometimes sprinkle warm water on him. Hermit crabs live in hard shells. When they grow, they need larger shells to move into."

4. An A+ answer: "Hermit crabs are easy to care for because you need only a few supplies and to feed them once a day. So, hermit crabs make great pets."

Did your child get the correct answers? If so, have your child explain what makes a good summary.

Did your child get any of the answers wrong? If so, explain to your child that a good summary includes only the most important details. Then, ask your child to pick out details he or she thinks are important and explain why. Check that your child understands that important details have a big effect on the meaning of the text.

Watch Out!

Summarizing can be challenging for third graders. Their summaries may include way too many details and be more like a book report. If you find that your child is including too much information in a summary, guide him or her to tell the most important details using only one to three sentences.

What to Know...

Kids may have trouble remembering what *summary* and *detail* mean because these are not words they often hear outside of school.

Review these skills with your child this way:

- A **detail** is a piece of information in a passage, sometimes given in a word or phrase.
- A **summary** is a retelling of the most important information in a passage or the main points of a story. A summary includes the topic, the major events, the main theme or ideas, or the most important characters. A summary is usually brief.

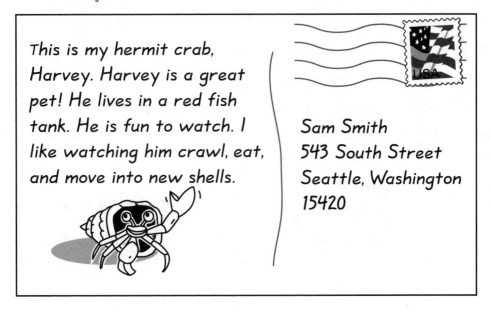

This is my hermit crab, Harvey. Harvey is a great pet! He lives in a red fish tank. He is fun to watch. I like watching him crawl, eat, and move into new shells.

Sam Smith
543 South Street
Seattle, Washington
15420

Kids should be able to recognize the following details in the postcard:

- The crab's name is Harvey.
- He lives in a fish tank.
- He is fun to watch.

Ask your child to identify details from the postcard. Tell your child to include details from the picture of the hermit crab.

When writing summaries, your kid might have a hard time deciding which details are the most important. Important details usually affect the meaning of a text more than less important details.

More important:

- Harvey is a great pet.
- Harvey lives in a fish tank.
- He is fun to watch.

Less important:

- The fish tank is red.
- It's fun to watch him crawl, eat, and move into new shells.

Explain to your child that the postcard tells the basics about Harvey. So, it's more important to know that Harvey lives in a fish tank than to know the color of the fish tank. Knowing the color of the fish tank doesn't change the meaning of the postcard.

The best summaries include the most important details. Look at these examples:

- Hermit crabs are fun to watch and make great pets.
- My friend has a great time watching her pet hermit crab, Harvey.

Ask your child to come up with a summary of the postcard in his or her own words. See if your child can summarize the postcard in one sentence.

Third Graders Are...

Third graders are often anxious about taking tests. To help them prepare for tests, they need plenty of chances to practice. Review skills in a non-threatening and fun way. Then, talk about how the skills might be presented on a test. Knowing what to expect can help your child feel more comfortable when test time arrives.

On Your Way to an "A" Activities

10 minutes

Type: Reading/Writing
Materials needed: paper, index cards, pencils
Number of players: 2 or more

Write a list of movies that all the players have seen. Then, each player should write a brief summary of each movie on an index card. Don't show each other your summaries! Then, read one summary aloud. See if another player can name the movie. Take turns reading your cards to each other and guessing the movies.

10 minutes

Type: Arts and Crafts
Materials needed: construction paper, paper, pencils, markers, glitter, glue, other art supplies
Number of players: 1

Think about your favorite book, movie, or story. Write a list of details from it. Then, make a poster by drawing pictures of each detail on the construction paper. Circle three details that you think are the most important. Then, in the center of the poster, write a summary in two or three sentences.

Has your child breezed through the activities? If so, he or she can work on this Using Your Head activity independently.

Using Your Head

{ **10** }
minutes

*Grab a **pencil** and some **crayons** or **markers**!*

Imagine you have a hermit crab for a pet. Cross out the details that you think are less important. Then, use the important details to write a summary in a postcard to a friend. Color the picture of the hermit crab!

Bright red	Drinks water	Doesn't like apples
Like to climb	Eats food	Bought at a pet store
Climbs on rocks and bowls	Likes bananas	Pet store was near my school

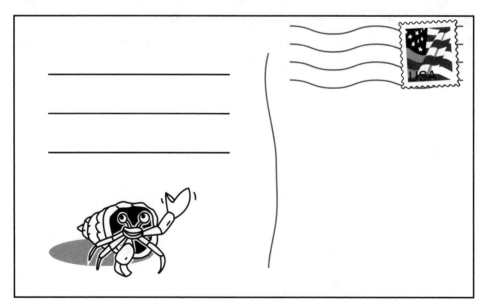

Answers: Less important details could be: climbs on rocks and bowls; likes bananas; doesn't like apples; pet store was near my school.

Using Illustrations

You know the saying "A picture is worth a thousand words." Well, years ago, your kid knew well the value of a picture from reading picture books. But your kid knows that grown-ups read books that are mostly words. To your kid, books with lots of words feel very grown-up. So, by third grade, your kid probably thinks of pictures as a thing for "baby books."

Your kid might get into the bad habit of ignoring the pictures or illustrations that come in a book. While focusing on the text may seem like breaking exciting new ground to your child, the pictures and illustrations often carry important info that's not in the text. Ignoring the pictures could leave your child in the dark. Your child needs to use the pictures to fully comprehend a passage. Make sure your kid remembers what pictures are worth.

First things first: Get a sense of what your kid already knows. Turn the page and tell your kid to Jump Right In!

Here's what you'll need for this lesson:
- *picture books*
- *paper*
- *crayons or markers*
- *pencils*

Jump Right In!

How to Make a Terrarium or Vivarium

Have you ever had a terrarium or a vivarium? They are fun and easy to make.

Step 1:	Get a container that you can see through, such as an old fish tank, an empty soda bottle, or an empty milk jug.
Step 2:	Put a layer of pebbles on the bottom.
Step 3:	Cover the pebbles with about two inches of dirt.
Step 4:	Add small plants or seeds. Also, add some rocks.
Step 5:	Add a little water to make everything slightly damp, but don't add too much water.
Step 6:	Close your terrarium with a cover or a bottle cap.

Put your terrarium in a place with a little sunlight. You can watch the water turn to mist and dew. You can also watch the plants grow!

A terrarium with small animals is called a vivarium. Make air holes in the terrarium. Add some small animals (like grasshoppers). Make sure you feed your animals or include plants that your animals can eat.

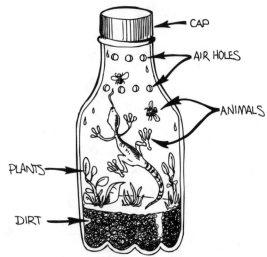

1. What type of container is used in the picture?

    A. fish tank

    B. soda bottle

    C. small jug

    D. shoe box

2. What could you learn from the vivarium in the picture?

    A. how rocks are formed

    B. how to start a garden

    C. how to care for fish

    D. how lizards catch insects

3. What types of animals could live in a vivarium? How do you know?

_____

_____

_____

4. Does the picture show a terrarium or a vivarium? How can you tell?

_____

_____

_____

_____

Excellent Job!

 **Checking In**

ⓐAnswers for page 53:

1. B

2. D

3. An A+ answer: "Grasshoppers, lizards, and bugs could live in a vivarium. The passage says small animals like grasshoppers could be added, and the picture shows a lizard and an insect."

4. An A+ answer: "The picture shows a vivarium. I can tell because it includes animals. The passage says that a terrarium with animals is called a vivarium."

Did your child get the correct answers? If so, ask your child to describe how the pictures relate to the steps.

Did your child get any of the answers wrong? If so, ask, "Why did you choose that answer?" Your child may have been hesitant to rely on the picture and instead used only information from the text. You might say, "The story talks about several containers that could be used, but let's look at the picture. What type of container does it show?"

 **Watch Out!**

Sometimes third graders are so used to hearing, "What does the story say?" and "Can you find the answer in the text?" that they are resistant to look for answers anywhere else. They need to be reminded that illustrations are more than just a decoration on the page. Illustrations contain information too. Explain to your child that sometimes the pictures contain information that the passage doesn't have. Ask your child to come up with reasons he or she might want to look at the pictures when answering questions.

What to Know...

Kids can get into the habit of overlooking illustrations when they read. But there is often a lot of important information included in pictures. Paying attention to illustrations, graphs, charts, maps, and captions can boost your kid's comprehension significantly.

Review these skills with your child this way:

- **Illustrations** often show a picture of topics and events from the passage. Strong readers often use illustrations to make sure they understand what is going on in the passage. They identify details in illustrations and answer questions based on the details in illustrations. Strong readers understand that illustrations and passages go hand in hand and that sometimes illustrations show details not mentioned in the passage.

Your child might see a poster in the neighborhood.

FREE!
My cat had babies. They are 4 weeks old. We can't keep them. We want to find a good home for them.

Call Don if you're interested at 555-1212.

Ask your child to identify a detail in the illustration that does *not* appear in the text. Also, ask your child to identify a detail from the text that does *not* appear in the illustration.

Kids should be able to connect the illustration to the text.

- The illustration shows that there are three kittens and that the kittens are black, white, and black and white. These details do not appear in the text.
- The text says that the kittens are 4 weeks old. This detail isn't in the illustration.

Third Graders Are...

By third grade, kids aren't just learning to read; they're beginning to read to learn. They're reading about American history, the solar system, dinosaurs, and other topics in school. They have to learn from what they read. Your kid will need to rely on ever more complicated illustrations. Encourage your kid to point out any illustrations he finds in nonfiction and informational texts, such as timelines, diagrams, photographs, etc. Ask your child to tell what he or she learned from the text, as well as from the illustrations.

On Your Way to an "A" Activities

{10 minutes}
Type: Reading/Writing
Materials needed: picture books
Number of players: 2 or more

Choose a book that is mostly pictures. Look at all the pictures in the book, but don't read the words. Using only the pictures, tell the story to the other players. Then, read the book together. Find out how close your story was to the actual story! Switch turns.

{15 minutes}
Type: Active
Materials needed: paper, pencil, crayons or markers
Number of players: 2 or more

With the other players, see how much information you can put into pictures. Draw a picture (don't show it). Try to include as many details as possible in your picture. For example, if you want to draw a picture of the beach, you could add details like seagulls, people, towels, sand castles, umbrellas, and so on. The other players should do the same. Trade pictures with another player. Then, point out all the details you see in each other's pictures. When you are both done, discuss what you saw in the pictures. Did you find all the details in the other player's picture? Did the other player find all the details in your picture?

Has your child breezed through the activities? If so, he or she can work on this Using Your Head activity independently.

Using Your Head

{ **10** minutes }

*Grab some **crayons** or **markers** and a **pencil**!*

Pete's Pet Store has classes teaching about animals. The chart below shows what classes Pete has planned for this weekend.

 **Pete's Pet Classes**

Time	Friday	Saturday	Sunday
9-11 a.m.	Terrariums	Turtles and Frogs	Your Pet Lizard
2-4 p.m.	Vivariums	Snakes!	Terrariums
6-8 p.m.	Your Pet Lizard	Vivariums	Reptiles

1. When are the terrarium classes scheduled?

_____

2. When can you learn about choosing a snake?

_____

3. Use crayons or colored pencils to do the following:

Color classes about terrariums blue.
Color classes about vivariums yellow.
Color classes that teach about animals green.

Answers: 1. Friday 9-11 a.m. and Sunday 2-4 p.m.; 2. Saturday 2-4 p.m.; 3. boxes labeled "Terrariums" should be blue; boxes labeled "Vivariums" should be yellow; remaining boxes should be green.

Fiction and Nonfiction

By third grade, kids are exposed to more and more types of reading texts. When they were younger, kids read a lot of fairy tales, stories, and other types of fiction. Mostly they read for fun. Now they are starting to read nonfiction texts, including textbooks, biographies, and magazine articles. They are reading these to learn and find information.

Sometimes, your kid may have trouble telling the difference between fiction and nonfiction. This might not seem like a big deal, but the type of text changes how your child will approach reading the text. Also, your kid might have different purposes in reading nonfiction than in reading fiction. Help your kid handle this new way of thinking about what he or she reads.

First things first: Get a sense of what your kid already knows. Turn the page and tell your kid to Jump Right In!

Here's what you'll need for this lesson:
- *pencil*
- *paper*
- *photographs*
- *books on a bookshelf*
- *crayons or markers*

 **Jump Right In!**

Our Solar System

We live on the planet Earth. Our planet is part of a solar system. There are other planets in our solar system. The center of the solar system is the sun.

The planets closest to the sun are called the inner planets. They are the hottest. The inner planets are Mercury, Venus, Earth, and Mars. They are fairly small, and they are rocky like Earth.

The next planets are the outer planets. They are colder. The outer planets are Jupiter, Saturn, Uranus, and Neptune. There is also something called Pluto. For years, scientists couldn't decide if Pluto was a planet. Right now, many scientists think it is not a planet. The debate could continue for years to come!

My Trip to Mars

My family takes the best vacations. Two summers ago, we went to Florida. Last summer, we went to Canada. This summer, we went to Mars. It was the best trip ever!

Mars is a planet next to Earth. It is too far to drive, and there are no roads. So, we rode on a rocket. We flew past stars and comets. Then, we landed on Mars. It is called the Red Planet and is about half the size of Earth. It is also colder than Earth because it is farther from the sun.

We put on our space suits, walked around, and collected rocks. We took a lot of pictures. Then, we got back on our rocket and came home. I can't wait for next summer's trip! Who knows where we'll go!

1. Which passage is nonfiction? How do you know?

_____

_____

_____

2. Write three things you learned from the nonfiction passage.

_____

_____

_____

3. Which passage is fiction? How do you know?

_____

_____

_____

4. Sometimes fiction contains facts. What facts did you read in the fiction passage?

_____

_____

_____

Excellent Job!

 *Checking In*

A Answers for page 61:

1. An A+ answer: "'Our Solar System' is nonfiction because it provides only facts. There's nothing made up in the passage."

2. An A+ answer: "I learned that the planets closest to the sun are called inner planets, are the hottest, are fairly small, and are rocky."

3. An A+ answer: "'My Trip to Mars' is fiction because it tells a made-up story about someone who goes to Mars on vacation."

4. An A+ answer: "The fiction passage said that Mars is a planet next to Earth, which is a fact. It also said that Mars is colder than Earth, which is also a fact."

Did your child get the correct answers? If so, ask your child to tell what details helped him or her decide whether the passages were fiction or nonfiction.

Did your child get any of the answers wrong? If so, discuss examples of nonfiction with your child, such as the dictionary, encyclopedias, and newspapers. Then, discuss examples of fiction with your child, such as novels, short stories, and plays. Then, ask your child to use this information to try to answer the questions again.

 Watch Out!

Sometimes third graders will mistake a fiction passage for nonfiction if it contains factual information, or even information that sounds like it might be true. Remind your child that for a passage to be fiction, the story must be made up, even if parts of it seem real or are true. For example, a story about a kid going to a park is fiction if the kid is a made-up kid, even though it's possible for a kid to go to a park.

What to Know...

Kids can get the terms *fiction* and *nonfiction* confused.

Review these skills with your child this way:

- **Fiction** is writing that tells a made-up story. Fiction tells a story with imagined characters and events. Stories and fairy tales are examples of fiction.
- **Nonfiction** is writing that tells only facts and true information. Textbooks are examples of nonfiction.

Your child might see these books in a book club magazine.

1

The Best Vacations! Facts, maps, tips, and more!

2

Take Me to Your Leader A green alien joins the third grade! Read what he tells the principal!

3

Pluto Club In science class, a group of friends makes a secret pact.

Ask your child to tell what he or she might read in each of the books.

Most kids can recognize the following information about fiction and nonfiction:

- *The Best Vacations!* is nonfiction because it contains only facts and information about vacations.
- *Take Me to Your Leader* is fiction because it tells a made-up story about an alien.
- *Pluto Club* is fiction. While it may include facts, it tells a made-up story about a group of friends.

 *Checking In*

If your child is a reluctant reader, you may find that nonfiction can grab your child's attention and interest. Take your child to a bookstore or library, and encourage your child to pick out books on topics that he or she finds interesting, such as books about a favorite race car driver, climbing the Himalayas, dinosaurs, or other topics.

Third Graders Are...

Third graders have very active imaginations. Sometimes, this makes it hard for them to tell the difference between fact and fiction. Help your child focus on what is real and what is make-believe. Talk about what makes them different. Be sure to praise your child's creativity and imagination.

On Your Way to an "A" Activities

5 minutes

Type: Reading/Writing
Materials needed: photographs, paper, pencil
Number of players: 2 or more

Find a photograph. Write a nonfiction sentence about the picture. This should be a fact or piece of information. Then, write a fiction sentence about the picture. This can be something imaginary or made up. Read your sentences aloud. The other players have to figure out which sentence is fiction and which is nonfiction. Then, take turns. Another player should find a photograph and write fiction and nonfiction sentences. You should decide which sentence is fiction and which is nonfiction.

15 minutes

Type: Active
Materials needed: books on a bookshelf
Number of players: 1 or more

Find a bookshelf with a lot of books. Sort them by fiction and nonfiction. Put all the fiction books on the left. Put all the nonfiction books on the right.

Has your child breezed through the activities? If so, he or she can work on this Using Your Head activity independently.

Using Your Head

[**10** minutes]

*Grab a **pencil** and some **crayons** or **markers**!*

Put the books on the right shelf! Fiction books are on the top shelf. Nonfiction books are on the bottom shelf. Read the book titles. Then, write the number of each book where it belongs.

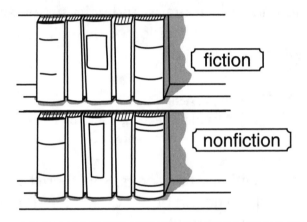

fiction

nonfiction

1. *Saturn, the Planet with Rings*

2. *The Cow Jumped Over the Moon*

3. *Learn About the Solar System*

4. *The Moon Is Made of Green Cheese*

5. *The Inner Planets*

6. *Jupiter, the Largest Planet*

7. *The Science Fair Mystery*

8. *An Astronaut Tells the Facts About the Moon*

9. *The Year I Felt Like an Alien*

10. *Who Turned Off the Sun?*

Answers: Top shelf: 2, 4, 7, 9, and 10; bottom shelf: 1, 3, 5, 6, and 8

Main Idea

Sometimes when you ask your child what a book, movie, or TV show was about, he or she might talk about one detail—a detail that has little to do with what happened in the rest of the story. Other times, your kid might retell the whole story. That's great that your kid can remember details so well and show his or her comprehension and memory skills. However, there are other times when your child needs to be able to pick out just the most important part.

It can be hard for kids to identify the main idea. Usually, this is a skill that they practice only at school. How many times in everyday life do you really ask, "What was the main idea of what happened while you were at your friend's house?" or "Tell me only the most important thing about your soccer tournament?"

To correctly identify a main idea, your child needs to be able to recognize when an author states the main idea. When the author doesn't state the main idea directly, your kid needs to be able to figure out the main idea by picking out important details.

First things first: Get a sense of what your kid already knows. Turn the page and tell your kid to Jump Right In!

Here's what you'll need for this lesson:
- *TV guide*
- *family photos or magazine photos*
- *paper*
- *pencil*

Jump Right In!

Cleaning Day

I'd looked forward all week
to a fun Saturday,
but Mom said, "Clean your room
before you can play."

"Fold your clean clothes,"
my dear mother said.
"Pick up the toys,
and make your bed."

"Get the puzzle pieces
and games off the floor,
put the books on the shelf,
hang your backpack on the door."

I cleaned, picked up, folded,
and put away as fast as I could.
And now I have to admit,
my room looks really good!

1. Which of these is the main idea of the poem?

   A. It was Saturday.

   B. I had to make the bed.

   C. I had to clean my room before I could play.

   D. It was time to fold all of my clean clothes.

2. Which of the following is a detail from the poem?

   A. My backpack was on the bed.

   B. There were games on the floor.

   C. My mom washed my clothes.

   D. I wanted to play soccer.

3. What are three details that tell how the room must have looked before it was cleaned up?

   _____

   _____

   _____

4. What is this poem mainly about? Use your own words.

   _____

   _____

   _____

Excellent Job!

 **Checking In**

Ⓐ Answers for page 69:

1. C

2. B

3. An A+ answer: "Before the room was clean, there were clothes to be folded, and the bed was not made. Puzzle pieces and games were on the floor. Toys needed to be picked up, and books needed to go on the shelf. Also, the backpack was not hung up."

4. An A+ answer: "This poem is about a kid who had to clean up his or her room before playing. In the end, the room looked good."

Did your child get the correct answers? If so, ask your child to write another stanza for this poem. Make sure your child includes details that support the main idea that the kid in the poem had to clean his or her room before playing, such as a detail about playing a game once the room was spotless.

Did your child get any of the answers wrong? If so, ask, "Why did you pick that answer?" Often, kids at this age have trouble choosing which idea is the most important. Your kid may recognize that all of the choices in question 1 included details from the poem. But, it could be hard to choose which is the main idea. Help your child by saying, "All of these contain details from the poem. Which one best tells what the whole poem was about?"

 **Watch Out!**

Third graders may confuse main idea and summary. Main idea is the one most important idea that the whole passage is mostly about. A summary retells the most important ideas in a few sentences. Help your child find the main idea by looking for one sentence in the passage that tells the most important idea. Often, this is in the first or last sentence, although it could be anywhere in the passage. At times, the main idea is not directly stated. In this case, ask your child to tell the most important idea in only one sentence.

What to Know...

In school, your child may hear main idea referred to as the "big idea." Both mean the same thing. What matters is that your kid recognizes the most important idea in a passage.

Review these skills with your child this way:

- A **main idea** is a statement of what a passage is mostly about. Often, an author states the main idea in the first or last sentences of the passage. An author may also choose not to state the main idea directly, in which case the reader has to infer the main idea of the passage.

- **Details** are bits of information in a passage, sometimes given in a word or a phrase. Regarding a main idea, a **supporting detail** is a detail from the passage that supports the main idea. Sometimes, there are details in a passage that contradict the main idea.

Your child might use details to figure out the main idea of a ripped set of instructions.

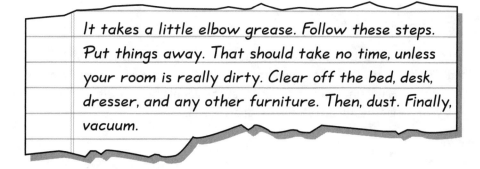

It takes a little elbow grease. Follow these steps. Put things away. That should take no time, unless your room is really dirty. Clear off the bed, desk, dresser, and any other furniture. Then, dust. Finally, vacuum.

Explain to your child that the first and last sentences are missing. Ask your kid to write a first sentence and last sentence in his or her own words.

Check out some possible main ideas.

Cleaning your room can be quick and easy.

It takes a little elbow grease. Follow these steps. Put things away. That should take no time, unless your room is really dirty. Clear off the bed, desk, dresser, and any other furniture. Then, dust. Finally, vacuum.

If you do things in this order, cleaning your room is a snap.

Watch Out!

Sometimes there are details in a passage that don't support a main idea. Ask your kid to identify the details that don't support the main idea that cleaning your room is quick and easy. Make sure your child sees that the details "a little elbow grease" and "unless your room is really dirty" don't support the main idea.

Study Right

Your child will need to organize the main idea and details when writing research reports or book reports. Using index cards can help. Discuss your child's favorite book or movie. Write ideas about the book or movie on separate index cards. Then, work together to group cards together that support certain main ideas. Organize the cards with details under the correct main idea. Show how the cards and ideas can then be used to plan writing the report. Your child can also do this on the computer.

Third Graders Are...

Some third graders may have a limited attention span. To keep your child's interest, practice skills several times, but keep each session relatively short. Not only is repeated practice over time an effective way to learn and reinforce skills, it also keeps your child from getting bored or distracted if a "study session" lasts too long.

On Your Way to an "A" Activities

10 minutes

Type: Game/Competitive
Materials needed: TV guide
Number of players: 2 or more

Think about a TV show all the players have seen this week. Each player should decide on the main idea of the show (don't share). Find the show in the TV guide. Read what it says about the show. Each player that came up with a main idea similar to the one in the TV guide gets a point. Now, play again by coming up with the main idea of a different show. See who earns the most points.

10 minutes

Type: Reading/Writing
Materials needed: photos of your family or from a magazine, paper, pencils
Number of players: 2 or more

Choose a photo. Work with the other players to come up with a main idea for the photo. For example, if it is a photo from a birthday party, you might say, "Everyone had a great time at the birthday party" as the main idea. Then, each player has to write down one detail that supports the main idea (for example, "The kid is smiling in front of the cake"). Next, each player has to write down one detail that doesn't support the main idea ("The kid in the background got cake in his hair and isn't smiling"). Finally, share your details with each other.

Has your child breezed through the activities? If so, he or she can work on this Using Your Head activity independently. If not, look for more main idea help at www.princetonreview.com/book.

Using Your Head

Grab a **pencil**!

Ling wrote what she did over the weekend. For each day, she wrote one main idea, a few supporting details, and one detail that doesn't support the main idea. Circle the main idea for each day. Cross out the detail that doesn't support the main idea.

Saturday	Sunday
We had fun playing football at the park.	We played four board games.
My brother was quarterback.	Tomorrow, it might be sunny.
We used my football.	We watched a movie.
We thought about playing basketball.	It was a rainy afternoon, so we stayed inside.

Answers: Saturday—Circle "We had fun playing football at the park," and cross out "We thought about playing basketball." Sunday—Circle "It was a rainy afternoon, so we stayed inside," and cross out "Tomorrow, it might be sunny."

Conclusions

When your child wakes up in the morning and notices dark clouds covering the sky and gusty winds blowing through the trees, he or she can probably figure out that there's a good chance of rain in the next couple hours. If you're having dinner at the local pizza parlor and notice a bunch of kids with party hats and balloons sitting at a gift-covered table, your child can probably figure out that someone is having a birthday party. In these cases, your child uses the obvious details to figure out a reasonable conclusion.

These same skills are used to draw conclusions while reading. To make conclusions, your kid must use the details in the passage. Your kid must think about what she is reading. Your kid must decide what details work together to support a conclusion, and what details don't.

Practicing making conclusions means your kid has to ask questions while reading and really get into the text. Not only does this mean your kid will be better at making conclusions and remembering details, but it also means that your kid will improve his or her reading comprehension skills.

First things first: Get a sense of what your kid already knows. Turn the page and tell your kid to Jump Right In!

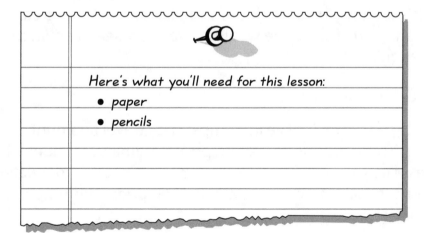

Here's what you'll need for this lesson:
- *paper*
- *pencils*

 **Jump Right In!**

A Whale of a Tale

How Whales Breathe

Whales are large animals. They live in the water. Some people think whales are fish, but fish breathe underwater through gills. Whales don't. Whales come to the surface of the water to breathe. Whales have lungs and breathe air, like we do.

Wow! That's Fin-tastic!

There are many kinds of whales. The biggest is the blue whale. Blue whales can grow to be over 90 feet long. That is the height of a 9-story building! That makes them the largest of all animals. The smallest whale is the dwarf sperm whale. They grow to only about eight-and-a-half feet long.

Whales eat tiny algae, plankton, and plants. Whales also eat small and large fish. Some whales have even been known to eat penguins!

Whale Communities

Many types of whales live in groups. They travel and hunt in these groups. These groups are called "pods." Animals that hunt whales are less likely to attack whales swimming in pods. Underwater, whales can "sing" to other whales in their pods. This is how they talk to each other.

1. Which of the following is the best conclusion for the section "Wow! That's Fin-tastic"?

    A. Whales' favorite food is plankton.

    B. Whales need to eat a lot of food.

    C. Whales eat different foods depending on the season.

    D. Whales eats lots of different types of food.

2. Whales that swim together in groups are most likely

    A. slower than whales that swim alone

    B. safer than whales that swim alone

    C. happier than other types of whales

    D. able to breathe more easily underwater

3. Are whales a kind of fish?

    _____

    _____

    _____

4. What details support your answer to question 3?

    _____

    _____

    _____

Excellent Job!

 **Checking In**

Answers for page 77:

1. D

2. B

3. An A+ answer: "Whales are not fish."

4. An A+ answer: "Fish breathe underwater, whereas whales have to come to the surface of the water to get air. Fish breathe through gills, whereas whales breathe air into their lungs."

Did your child get the correct answers? If so, have your child point out the details from the passage that helped her come to the correct conclusions. Ask your child to explain how she used the details to identify the correct answer.

Did your child get any of the answers wrong? Maybe he made a conclusion based on his personal thoughts or opinions on whales, rather than relying only on supporting details in the passage. Review each question. For question 1, you could say, "Let's find all of the information in the passage about what whales eat. We'll underline these details and use them to answer question 1." You could also review each answer choice and point out how the wrong answer choices are not supported. For example, the passage does mention that whales eat plankton, but doesn't say this is their favorite food—so answer choice A is incorrect.

 **Watch Out!**

Third graders may base conclusions on personal experiences or their own imaginations, rather than relying on supporting details from the text. For example, because whales spend their entire lives in the water, have fins, and swim, your child may assume they are fish. Remind your child that conclusions must be based on details in the text. Help her to stay focused on the information in the passage by asking questions such as, "Which details helped you come to that conclusion?" or "What part of the story supports what you said?"

What to Know...

Your kid might hear the terms *detail* and *conclusion* only during reading class in school. Help your child feel more familiar with these terms by using them at home and in a variety of situations.

Review these skills with your child this way:

- A **conclusion** is an idea or thought based on details in a passage.

- **Details** are bits of information in a passage, sometimes given in a word or phrase. When you make a conclusion about a passage, you base it on the details in the passage.

Your child may make more conclusions outside of school than he or she realizes. Imagine that you and your child find the following description and diagram at an aquarium or marine park while on vacation.

Beluga Whale

Beluga means "white one" in Russian. They don't eat plants or algae like some other whales. They live in pods of about 10 belugas. At times, several pods may travel together. This can mean that there are between 200 and 10,000 members in their group.

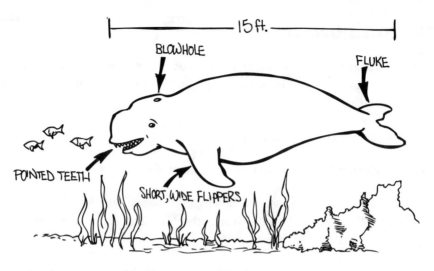

15 ft.

BLOWHOLE

FLUKE

POINTED TEETH

SHORT, WIDE FLIPPERS

Ask your child to describe what conclusions she can make based on the passage and the diagram.

Most kids can use the details in the passage and diagram to make these conclusions:

- The beluga is white in color.

- They eat only other fish and ocean animals.

Children struggle when they draw conclusions that are not supported by the details in the text or diagram. As a result, kids may come up with incorrect conclusions like these:

- The beluga is a fish.

- Beluga whales live only off the coast of Russia.

- Belugas live only in marine parks.

Third Graders Are...

Third graders sometimes have a hard time remembering lists of related details. Play this game to give your child practice. Say a sentence, such as, "I looked in Grandma's treasure chest and saw an (item beginning with 'a,' such as 'apple')." Then, ask your child to repeat what you said and to add an item beginning with the next letter. He might say, "I looked in Grandma's treasure chest and I saw an apple and a basket." Continue taking turns, seeing how far through the alphabet you can get before making a mistake. Praise your child for his efforts and for improvements in listening skills.

On Your Way to an "A" Activities

10 minutes

Type: Active
Materials needed: none
Number of players: 2 or more

Play "20 questions." Think of an object, an animal, a type of food, or something else. Then, another player can ask you 20 "yes or no" questions. You can answer only "yes" or "no" to the questions. The other player needs to gather details by asking questions to figure out what you have in mind. For example, if you are thinking of an octopus and the player asks, "Does it have 2 legs?" you would say "no." Once the other player correctly identifies what you had in mind, switch roles.

30 minutes

Type: Game/Competitive
Materials needed: paper and pencils
Number of players: 2 or more

Play the game "Charades." Think of a person you all know. Write the person's name on a piece of paper and list details that would show who the person is. Then, "perform" those details, acting like the person—no talking! The other players have to guess who the person is. Once they have guessed correctly, switch roles.

Has your child breezed through the activities? If so, he or she can work on this Using Your Head activity independently. If not, look for more conclusions help at www.princetonreview.com/book.

Using Your Head

{ 10 minutes }

*Grab a **pencil**!*

Read the conclusions and details below. Circle two details that support each conclusion. Then, cross out the detail that does not support each conclusion.

1. Whales do not stay underwater all the time.
   A. They come to the surface for air.
   B. They poke their heads out of the water.
   C. They eat underwater.

2. Whales "sing" to help each other.
   A. They sing to talk to friends.
   B. They sing to the fish they eat.
   C. They sing to their babies.

Answers: 1. Circle A and b, and cross out C. 2. Circle A and C, and cross out B.

Cracking the Third Grade

Plot and Setting

There are times when your kid can talk and talk, telling you all sorts of wild details. Maybe you've asked your kid what a movie was about—and suddenly your kid plunged into a litany about dinosaurs, car chases, and a hilarious scene involving cheese. At the end, you still can't put your finger on exactly what happened in the movie. Your child has told you nearly everything, yet not the few key details you were looking for.

When figuring out the plot or the setting of a story, your child needs to be able to hone in on specific details. To figure out the setting, your child has to be able to pick out the details that describe where and when the story took place. To figure out the plot, your child needs to know which details are the most important (not just the funniest, the grossest, or the ones involving chase scenes).

First things first: Get a sense of what your kid already knows. Turn the page and tell your kid to Jump Right In!

Here's what you'll need for this lesson:

- paper
- pencils
- shoe box(es)
- colored markers
- colored paper
- clock or timer
- art supplies, such as glue, scissors, felt, scrap material, leaves, cotton, pipe cleaners, sparkles, etc.

 **Jump Right In!**

The Middle of Nowhere

Vince and his mom decided to take a bus to their favorite restaurant—Sippin' Savory Soups. They got to the bus stop just as a bus was pulling away.

"Wait!" his mother yelled. Luckily, the bus driver stopped. Vince and his mom ran onto the bus.

Vince watched his neighborhood pass by through the window. After they had been riding for a while, Vince started to see unfamiliar places.

"Where are we?" Vince asked. His mom said that they must have taken the wrong bus.

"We're in the middle of nowhere!" Vince cried. "What if we never find our way home?" His mother spoke to the driver, and Vince tried not to worry. Just then, they passed a playground. Kids were playing on a shiny, curvy slide. Vince had never seen one like it.

Vince and his mom got off at the next bus stop and took a new bus. In no time, they had arrived at their soup restaurant in time for dinner. The restaurant was full of people sipping soups.

"Happy to be in a place you know?" his mom asked.

"Yes," Vince said, "but can we go to the playground with the curvy slide sometime?"

"You mean the one in the middle of nowhere?" his mother asked. They laughed and then hungrily sipped their favorite soups.

1. What is the most important thing that happened in the story?

    A. The bus was pulling away from the bus stop.

    B. Many people were in the restaurant.

    C. Vince and his mom were hungry.

    D. Vince and his mom took the wrong bus.

2. Where is Vince when he sees the curvy slide?

    A. at Sippin' Savory Soups

    B. on the wrong bus

    C. at a playground

    D. at home

3. At the end of the story, where was Vince?

    _____

    _____

4. What details in the story tell you where Vince was at the end?

    _____

    _____

Excellent Job!

Checking In

Answers for page 85:

1. D

2. B

3. An A+ answer: "Vince was at Sippin' Savory Soups."

4. An A+ answer: "The story says that Vince and his mom saw a lot of people in the restaurant and they were hungrily sipping their own soups."

Did your child get the answers correct? If so, ask your child to explain *how* he or she arrived at one of the correct answers. If this poses difficulty, guide your child to the paragraph that provides a clear clue to the correct answer. You can also emphasize that setting is both the time and place where something happens. Ask your child to identify when Vince and his mom got to the restaurant.

Did your child get any of the answers wrong? If so, ask your child to rephrase what the question is asking. Make sure your child understands the question.

Watch Out!

Third graders sometimes confuse where a character is with where they are. For example, for question 2, your child might think Vince was at home when he saw the slide because your child was at home when he or she read about Vince. Reword the question, and ask your child, "Where is Vince in the story when he sees the curvy slide?"

What to Know...

Kids might get overwhelmed when asked to pick out certain details from a story. So much happened! But this is a skill your child can develop with practice.

Review these skills with your child this way:

- The **plot** is the series of events in a fictional story.

- The **setting** is the time and place in which the events in a fictional story take place.

When figuring out the plot of a story, your child needs to identify the important events that take place.

Important Events

- Vince and his mom took the wrong bus.
- Vince and his mom changed busses.
- Vince and his mom had soup.

Ask your child if the story would have changed a lot or a little if Vince and his mom had not changed busses. Make sure your child understands that changing important details would change the story a lot.

Less Important Events

- Vince's mom yelled, "Wait!"
- People ate soup at the restaurant.
- Vince asked to go back to the playground.

Ask your child if the story would have changed a lot or a little if Vince didn't ask to go back to the playground. Make sure your child understands that changing less important details would not change the story much.

In the story, Vince was in a few places.

Ask your child to identify where Vince is in the first picture. Then, ask your child to identify where Vince is in the column of three pictures. Finally, ask your child to identify where Vince is in the last picture. Make sure your child can name that Vince was at a bus stop, on busses, and at a restaurant.

 Checking In

Your kid might get confused by where Vince is and what Vince sees. Point to the column of three pictures in the middle. Ask, "Vince sees a playground. Is he on the playground or is he in a bus?" and "There's a restaurant seen in the bus window. At this moment, is Vince in the restaurant or on the bus?"

 Study Right

Drawing pictures is a great way to study. Ask your child to draw a small picture that shows what happened in each paragraph of the story. By drawing pictures, your child represents details in an easy-to-use way. Your child can look at these pictures to determine the most important events and the setting.

On Your Way to an "A" Activities

30 minutes

Type: Arts and Crafts
Materials needed: shoe box(es), glue, scissors, colored markers, colored paper, felt, scrap material, leaves, cotton, pipe cleaners, sparkles, etc.
Number of players: 1 or more

Make a list of different settings. Use the following examples or come up with your own: walking to school in the rain, nighttime in your bedroom, a picnic in the park in summertime. Stand the shoe box on its side so that the open part faces you. Using your arts and crafts supplies, create a diorama that shows the setting of your choice. Be sure to provide clues that show both time and place. You can use cotton to make clouds or snow, leaves and pipe cleaners to make trees, and sparkles to make stars for nighttime settings.

15 minutes

Type: Speaking/Listening
Materials needed: a clock or timer
Number of players: 2 or more

Think of a story. It can be a story from a book, a movie, or a TV show. Tell the story to the other players in 3 minutes or less. When you are done, the other players have to try to tell the plot of the story in 1 minute or less. Take turns being the storyteller.

Has your child breezed through the activities? If so, he or she can work on this Using Your Head activity independently.

Using Your Head

{ **15** minutes }

*Grab a **pencil**!*

Go back to the story "The Middle of Nowhere" on page 84.

1. Read the beginning of the story again. Then, write only the *most important event* from the beginning of the story.

_____

_____

2. Now, read the middle of the story again. Write only the *most important event* from the middle of the story.

_____

_____

3. Now, read the end of the story again. Write only the *most important event* from the end of the story.

_____

_____

Answers: 1. Vince and his mom decided to go to Sippin' Savory Soups and almost missed the bus. 2. Vince and his mom realized that they were in the wrong place because they took the wrong bus. 3. Vince and his mom took another bus and got to the restaurant.

Character

For third graders, trying to describe a character in a story might seem like a vague and slippery task. When asked which details best identify a character, your child might think any number of details could apply equally well. Your child can learn to identify and describe characters by looking for clues to how the character acts, thinks, and feels in a story.

Chances are your child already knows more about characters than he or she realizes. Every day, your kid encounters people and sizes them up. On the bus, your child might see a boy wearing a baseball jacket for a certain team. "I wonder if he likes that team?" your child wonders. The boy's behavior—that he wears a team jacket—provides a clue that your child uses to make an initial guess about what the boy is like. Later that day, your child hears the boy talking about watching his favorite baseball team. Now, your kid has observed the boy's behavior on two separate occasions. Using many clues helps your child accurately have a sense of characters.

First things first: Get a sense of what your kid already knows. Turn the page and tell your kid to Jump Right In!

Here's what you'll need for this lesson:
- old magazines, catalogs, and newspapers
- heavy paper or cardboard
- crayons or markers
- scissors
- glue
- paper
- pencils

 **Jump Right In!**

The Perfect Crazy Summer Fort

As soon as the school year was over, Sebastian and Carlos decided to build a fort. They built it in Carlos's backyard. They worked all afternoon. They also made a flag out of a pole and a purple polka-dotted scarf.

"This is the most awesome fort ever!" Carlos exclaimed proudly. Sebastian had a very glum look on his face.

"We shouldn't have painted the door green," Sebastian said. "I have to fix it."

If Carlos didn't know Sebastian, he might have thought his friend was mad at him. However, he knew his friend very well. Sebastian was never happy right away with things he made. He always worked to make things better. Carlos liked that his friend worked so hard, but he knew they wouldn't have enough time to finish today.

When Sebastian's older sister came to pick him up, Sebastian was still busy painting the door red and fixing things. He had started to make a sign that said "Our Fort."

"Sorry, Carlos," Sebastian said. "I was hoping to finish before I left."

"It's okay, Sebastian," Carlos said. "I think it would be fun to work on the fort and play in it all summer long."

That made Sebastian grin from ear to ear. "Awesome!" he said. "So we can spend the summer making the most perfect crazy fort ever!"

1. Sebastian can best be described as a person who
   A. likes to paint
   B. wants everything to be perfect
   C. just wants to have fun
   D. often gets angry at his friends

2. Sebastian paints the door red because
   A. he thinks a red door is better than a green door
   B. he is angry with Carlos for painting the door green
   C. he wants to make Carlos proud of him
   D. he does not want to play with Carlos

3. How does Carlos know that Sebastian is <u>not</u> mad at him?

   _____

   _____

4. What is one way that Carlos and Sebastian are <u>not</u> alike?

   _____

   _____

Excellent Job!

 *Checking In*

Answers for page 93:

    1. B

    2. A

    3. An A+ answer: "Carlos knows that Sebastian wasn't angry because he's known Sebastian for a while. He's seen Sebastian work to make things better before."

    4. An A+ answer: "Carlos is happy with the fort, but Sebastian is not."

Did your child get the answer correct? If so, make sure your child understands Sebastian's character. Ask your child to point out all the details about Sebastian, including what he says and what he does.

Did your child choose any of the wrong answers? For question 1, your child might have chosen answer choice A because Sebastian painted the door. Ask your child, "When Sebastian painted the door again, was that because he liked to paint or because he wants the fort to be perfect?" Ask your kid to underline the things that Sebastian says, does, feels, and thinks in the story. Then, point out the correct answer and ask, "Can you see how this answer fits the details you underlined about Sebastian's character?"

 *Watch Out!*

Kids might feel that a question is unfair because more than one answer *could* describe a character. For example, with question 2, your child might have guessed answer choice C because Sebastian apologized to Carlos for not finishing. Tell your child that the best answer is supported by the details in the story. While answer choice C may seem possible, there aren't any details that support it. Sebastian says, "We shouldn't have painted the door green," which is a detail that supports answer choice A.

What to Know...

Your child works to understand characters all the time: when reading books, when watching movies, and even when hanging out with friends.

Review this skill with your child this way:

- **Characters** are the people whose actions, ideas, thoughts, and feelings a passage tells us about. Characters aren't always human. Sometimes animals, plants, or parts of the setting may be characters in a passage. Authors reveal character through details about the character, including what the character says and how the character behaves.

Your kid thinks about characters when reading a list of TV shows for kids.

Wiggly and Pals. Come join the adventures of Wiggly the Worm as he digs his way through Earth and learns about different places. This time, he digs under the sea, but Wiggly can't breathe underwater. Will Wiggly go back or figure out a way to explore the ocean?

Treehouse Tales. One day, Sarah could suddenly speak with the trees. Ever since, she and her classmates have worked to save the rain forests. This time, something mysterious is hurting her leafy friends. The fun-loving Sarah gets down to some serious business.

Stormcloud Thunderstrike. Devon sees the Thunderstrike symbol in the clouds. Whenever this happens, Devon always rushes to save the city. This time, he's frozen with fear. What kind of danger could be causing Devon to freeze?

Ask your child to underline as many characters as she can find in the descriptions of the shows. Remind her that the characters can be humans, plants, or animals.

Your child uses what he or she knows about characters to understand stories, movies, and books. A character might be happy in one scene and angry in the next. Does this make the character a happy person or an angry person? Your kid needs to look for clues to how a character feels, thinks, and acts throughout a story.

Most kids might describe the characters in the following ways:

- Wiggly is adventurous. He likes to explore.

- Sarah is hardworking and playful.

- Devon has courage and is helpful.

· · · · · · · · · · · · · ●
Ask your kid to describe the characters using the details in the television show descriptions.

Some kids might describe the characters based on one detail instead of on many details. If your kid described the characters based on one detail, he or she may have mistakenly described them in these ways:

- Wiggly doesn't like a challenge.

- Sarah is starting a new business.

- Devon is cold.

· · · · · · · · · · · · · ●
If your kid made a mistake and based her description on just one detail, ask her to think about how the character acts overall.

Third Graders Are...

Kids in third grade sometimes assume that everyone thinks and feels the exact same way that they do. So, when describing a character, they might describe a character based on their *own* feelings and thoughts in a similar situation. Look for opportunities to show your child that sometimes people have thoughts and feelings that *differ* from your child's thoughts and feelings.

On Your Way to an "A" Activities

{ 30 minutes }

Type: Arts and Crafts
Materials needed: old magazines, catalogs, newspapers, heavy paper or cardboard, crayons or markers, scissors, glue
Number of players: 1 or more

Draw a person's face on heavy paper or cardboard. Draw a thought balloon coming out of the person's mouth, like in a cartoon. Next, cut out parts of people's faces from magazines, catalogs, and/or newspapers. Arrange these parts on the blank face to make a new face. What kind of a character is this? Ask yourself: What is something that *only this character* might say? Cut out the letters and words in the magazines, catalogs, and newspapers. Arrange them in the thought bubble. When you've made a few different faces, you can glue your pieces down and hang up the portrait you've made!

{ 20 minutes }

Type: Game/Competitive
Materials needed: paper and pencil
Number of players: 3 or more

Each player makes a list describing a person all the players know. Each player takes a turn reading aloud from his or her list. The others guess who is being described. The first player to guess correctly gets a point. Keep playing until all the players have a turn reading their lists. Then, count up the points to see who wins!

Has your child breezed through the activities? If so, he or she can work on this Using Your Head activity independently.

Using Your Head

[10 minutes]

Grab a pencil!

Sebastian went back to Carlos's house. It was raining, so they made cookies instead of working on the fort. Here are some of the things they said. Draw a line from what was said to the character you think said it.

A. If we'd put nuts in the cookies, they would have been better.

B. I'm tired of trying to make every cookie perfectly round. Let's eat!

Sebastian

C. I know we forgot the nuts, but I like the cookies anyway.

Carlos

D. I don't care how hard it is or how long it takes, I'm going to keep trying to make these cookies perfectly round.

Putting Events in Order

Most third graders benefit from structure, both at home and at school. Your kid is probably used to structure—rules for playing in the house, steps for crossing the street, a ritual for brushing his teeth and washing his ears, and so on. Kids are used to being told what to do, when, and how. Instructions often come as a sequence of tasks (sit down, open your textbook, turn to page 20).

But as you know, not everything in the world is so clear—least of all in the stories, books, and newspaper articles we read.

Where reading is concerned, it's important for your child to learn how to identify and sort out a sequence of events from a collection of details in a text. Your kid needs to practice being able to determine the sequence of events on his or her own.

First things first: Get a sense of what your kid already knows. Turn the page and tell your kid to Jump Right In!

Here's what you'll need for this lesson:
- *a cookbook or magazine with recipes*
- *newspaper*
- *scissors*
- *pencils*
- *paper*

Jump Right In!

Egg Salad

Ingredients:

> 6 large eggs
> 2 tablespoons mayonnaise
> 1 teaspoon mustard
> Bread
> Salt and pepper, to taste

1. Put the eggs in a pot. Cover with cold water. Ask an adult to boil the eggs for 10 minutes. Then, ask an adult to drain the hot water and put the eggs in a bowl.

2. Cover the eggs with cold water. You can even add ice.

3. After the eggs have cooled, peel them carefully. Throw away the eggshells. Rinse the eggs to make sure no pieces of eggshell are left on them.

4. Mash the eggs with a fork.

5. Add the other ingredients. Mix. Taste the mixture using a clean spoon, then add more salt or pepper if you like.

6. Now you're ready to make sandwiches! Spread the egg salad on bread. You can save the rest of it for later. Just put it into a bowl with a cover, and keep it in the refrigerator!

1. What should you do <u>before</u> peeling the eggs?

    A. Mash them with a fork.

    B. Cool them in cold water.

    C. Add the mayonnaise.

    D. Put them in a pot of water to boil.

2. What should you do <u>after</u> adding the other ingredients?

    A. Rinse off the pieces of eggshells.

    B. Put it into a bowl with an airtight lid.

    C. Taste with a clean spoon.

    D. Mash them with a fork.

3. What is something you should do <u>before</u> peeling the eggs?

_____

_____

_____

4. What is something you should do <u>after</u> making sure the egg salad tastes good?

_____

_____

_____

Excellent Job!

 **Checking In**

❹Answers for page 101:

1. B

2. C

3. An A+ answer: "A parent should cook them, and I should cool them in a bowl of water and ice."

4. An A+ answer: "I should make a sandwich or put the egg salad in a covered container in the refrigerator."

Did your child get the answers correct? If so, ask your child to explain why the wrong answers are incorrect.

Did your child choose any of the wrong answers? If so, say, "Did you think about what would happen if you tried to peel the eggs at another point in the recipe?" Make sure your child has thought about how important it is to follow the sequence of events as laid out in the recipe.

 **Watch Out!**

Sometimes kids get confused about the order of events when certain details are talked about in different ways in a passage. For example, in the ingredients list, your child can see "mayonnaise" listed. Later, the recipe says to add the "other ingredients," which includes the mayonnaise. Did your child become confused about when to add the mayonnaise because it was referred to as "other ingredients"? If so, ask your child to act out the steps in the passage or imagine acting out the steps. This can help your child identify areas of confusion and clarify.

What to Know...

Sometimes kids have problems inferring the sequence of events. They're used to being told what to do next and reading stories that clearly say the order of events.

Review this skill with your child this way:

- **Sequence** is the order of ideas and events in a passage. The sequence in which events are presented in a passage may not be the same as the order in which the events described actually took place. Your kid can describe sequence using the words *before* and *after*.

> Today, Tanya is happy. She is happy because she remembered that her brother's birthday is tomorrow. Now she and her father will have time to bake him an excellent cake. Last year, Tanya didn't have time to make a cake because she forgot all about his birthday.

Ask your child to point to clues that tell about the order of events, such as "Now" and "Last year." Point out that the passage doesn't list the events in the order in which they happened.

Events in the order the passage talked about them:

- Today, Tanya remembered that her brother's birthday is tomorrow.
- She plans to make him a cake.
- She didn't make him a cake last year.
- She forgot her brother's birthday last year.

Events in the order they happened:

- Tanya forgot her brother's birthday last year.
- She didn't make him a cake last year.
- Today, she remembered that her brother's birthday is tomorrow.
- She plans to make him a cake.

 ## Study Right

Research shows that kids who grow up in homes where the family spends time reading are more likely to have positive attitudes about reading. Think about what you like to read and see if you can make the time for reading on a weekly basis. Talk to your child about what you're reading, why you're reading it, and what you like or dislike about it.

On Your Way to an "A" Activities

30 minutes

Type: Active
Materials needed: pencils and paper
Number of players: 2 or more

Play a treasure hunt game. Each player picks something that can be found nearby. Then, each player writes the name of the thing on a piece of paper and instructions for how to find the thing. For example, if you're playing in a house, you might pick a hairbrush. Then, you'd write "Hairbrush" and steps like "go down the hall, open the door on the left to my bedroom, go to the table." Do this for 4 more things that can be found nearby. So, in the end, each player should have picked 5 things and written 5 sets of instructions. Next, players trade instructions. Each player follows the instructions to find the things. Who wrote the best instructions? Who was able to find the most things?

15 minutes

Type: Speaking/Listening
Materials needed: a cookbook or magazine with recipes, pencils, paper
Number of players: 2 or more

Each player picks a recipe and rewrites it, mixing up the order in which things are prepared. Players then exchange mixed-up recipes and rewrite the other's mixed-up recipe, but list what to do in proper order. As the player makes the list, the recipe writer gives hints, saying things like, "You beat the eggs <u>after</u> melting the chocolate, but <u>before</u> you add the flour."

Type: Reading/Writing
Materials needed: a newspaper and scissors
Number of players: 2 or more

Play "What Happened?" Each player should find a story in a newspaper. Players should not read their own stories. Instead, players should read each other's stories and then return them. Next, cut your story into parts, making sure to cut around the words. Then, mix up the pieces of paper. Try to put the story back together. When you and the other player are done, check each other's work. See if all the events are in the correct order!

Type: Game/Competitive
Materials needed: pencil and paper
Number of players: 2 or more

Play "Fast forward/Rewind." Write a paragraph describing something you did. Write down each step as soon as it pops into your head, but not in order you did it. Use the phrases "before that" and "after that" to describe when you did each step. For example, you could write. "I took a bath. Before that, I did homework. After my bath, I put on my pajamas." Hand your paragraph to another player. The other player needs to figure out the actual order of the steps you took. Then, the other player should act out the correctly ordered steps. Take turns. Now, another player should write a paragraph. Then, you can figure out the correct order and act out the paragraph.

Using Your Head

{ **10** minutes }

*Grab a **pencil**!*

Julie and her older brother plan to surprise their parents with a huge pancake breakfast. They wrote a list of everything they have to do, but the dog chewed it.

Help them put the list back in order. Write the letter of each step in order below.

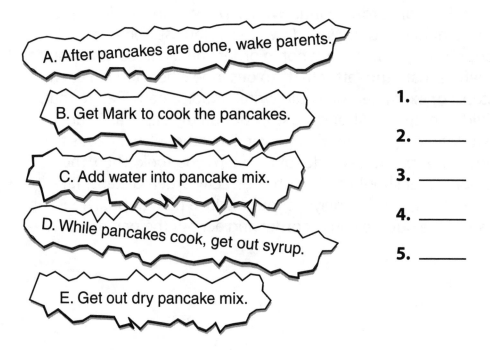

A. After pancakes are done, wake parents.

B. Get Mark to cook the pancakes.

C. Add water into pancake mix.

D. While pancakes cook, get out syrup.

E. Get out dry pancake mix.

1. _____

2. _____

3. _____

4. _____

5. _____

Answers: 1. E; 2. C; 3. B; 4. D; 5. A

Problem and Solution

A story's problem is not always easy to spot for your third grader. Stories rarely say straight out, "This is the central problem in the story" or "This is how the problem got solved." Because of this, a third grader might think that there are many problems in a story, or that there are no problems in the story at all.

Your kid needs to know that all stories have a central problem. Problems often come up between two characters in a story, but there are other kinds of problems too. A problem can occur in a story when a character comes into conflict with an obstacle in nature or society. In some stories, like mysteries, the problem is often that a character does not know something that is important to solving a case. The case (and the problem) is solved when the character finds out the thing that he or she didn't know at the beginning of the story. All stories, whether they are mysteries or not, contain details that your kid can use as clues to identify the story's problem and to understand its solution.

First things first: Get a sense of what your kid already knows. Turn the page and tell your kid to Jump Right In!

Here's what you'll need for this lesson:
- pencils
- paper
- superhero comics
- crayons and markers
- art supplies

Jump Right In!

Race Against the Rain

Zelda and Paul went camping with their mom and dad. They brought along their dog, Doodad. The family had so much fun hiking and playing in the woods all day that they didn't notice the storm clouds gathering in the sky. At last they realized that if they didn't act soon, they were going to get very, very wet. They rushed back to their campsite and set to work.

Each member of the family helped. Paul put away the leftovers from lunch. He checked the backpacks to make sure there were enough warm clothes for everyone to take into the tent. He gathered flashlights and a lantern. Zelda raked pine needles into a pile, then spread them out evenly to make the ground soft in the place where the tent would go. Then, Mom, Dad, Zelda, and Paul worked together to put up their tent. Even Doodad did his part. He danced around in circles, barking, reminding everyone to hurry. The rain is on its way! The rain is coming!

Finally, after all the backpacks and supplies had been put into the tent, they all crawled inside. Just as Paul zipped the tent flap closed, they heard a thunderclap. A few seconds later, it started to rain outside. Dad unrolled the sleeping bags. Zelda turned on the lantern. Then, they took turns telling stories. After that, no one said anything for a while. They just listened to the rain going *thwap! thwap! thwap!* against their tent. Then, one by one, Paul, Zelda, Mom, Dad, and Doodad fell asleep.

Cracking the Third Grade

1. The problem in this story is that
   A. they realize they shouldn't have brought Doodad
   B. Paul and Zelda both want to put up the tent
   C. Zelda is afraid of rainstorms
   D. it is going to rain and the campsite isn't ready

2. The problem in the story is solved because
   A. everybody takes turns telling stories
   B. Doodad warns them that it is going to rain
   C. everyone rushes to get the campsite ready
   D. they leave the campsite and go to a motel

3. How do you know that the problem is solved at the end of the story?

   _____

   _____

   _____

   _____

   _____

Excellent Job!

 **Checking In**

Ⓐ Answers for page 109:

1. D

2. C

3. An A+ answer: "At the end of the story, the family is able to get inside the tent before it starts to rain."

Did your child get the answers correct? If so, ask your child to tell you which details in the story helped lead to the correct answers. This will reinforce for your child that a story's problem and solution can always be found in a story's details.

Did your child get any of the answers wrong? If so, ask your child to point out a detail in the story that led to that answer. For question 2, your child may have guessed that the problem in the story was solved because everybody took turns to tell a story inside the tent. Say, "It's true that *after* the problem was solved, everybody told stories, but does telling stories help keep them from getting wet?"

 **Watch Out!**

Third graders sometimes follow their likes and dislikes instead of paying close attention to the details of a passage. For instance, if your child is frightened by rainstorms, he or she may have thought the answer to question 1 was that Zelda was afraid of rainstorms—even though this isn't supported by the details in the story. Or, for question 2, if your child doesn't like to camp, he or she may have picked the answer choice saying that the family solved the problem by going to a motel. Remind your child that the correct answer is supported by the details in the passage.

What to Know...

Your kid can learn to identify problems in a story by looking for details that express conflict. Your kid might describe problems and conflicts in stories as "when things got hard," "when the characters didn't know what to do," or "when I didn't know what would happen next."

Review this skill with your child this way:

- A **problem** in a passage may be between a character and another character, between a character and society, between a character and nature, or between a character and himself or herself. Sometimes there is a problem between opposing groups of characters.

With your kid, read this story in which different problems and solutions occur.

Drey and Rachel wanted to play, but it was too hot.

"I wish we had some shade in our backyard," Drey said.

"Yeah," Rachel agreed. "Someplace nice and cool."

So Drey and Rachel decided to make their own fort. They knew they needed sticks and lots of fabric. Rachel searched for sticks, and Drey searched for fabric. Rachel found sticks in her neighbor's yard. She asked him if she could use them, but her neighbor said no. So, Rachel found some old broomsticks in the basement. Drey knew they kept extra fabric and rags in the house, but he couldn't remember where. Instead, he found some old bedsheets. The broomsticks and the bedsheets worked perfectly! They made a large and shady fort—a perfect place to play games in the summer heat!

Ask your child to identify the problems in this passage.

Most kids can identify the following problems and solutions in the story:

Problem	Type of Problem	Solution
It was too hot to play	Character vs. Nature	Drey and Rachel decided to make a fort
Rachel couldn't use the sticks she found	Character vs. Character	Rachel used broomsticks
Drey couldn't remember where the fabric was	Character vs. Self	Drey used old bedsheets

· · · · · · · · · · · · ●

Ask your kid to give you examples of different types of conflicts from his or her life or from stories in books, magazines, or movies.

On Your Way to an "A" Activities

20 minutes

Type: Active
Materials needed: pencil, paper, superhero comic books
Number of players: 4 or more

Play "Superheroes, Superhumans!" Form teams of 2 or more players. Each team picks a superhero and a problem. You can look for one in a comic book. Now, each team acts out the problem and acts out how the superhero solved the problem. Then, the team has to act out a way a regular human could solve the problem without superpowers. For example, if Superman saw a person stuck on the top of a mountain, he might fly to save the person. A regular human might have to climb the mountain or take a helicopter! Each team takes a turn acting out a problem and solution with a favorite superhero!

30 minutes

Type: Arts and Crafts
Materials needed: paper, crayons or markers, art supplies
Number of players: 2 or more

Play "Crazy Problems." With the other players, make up a story by listing crazy problems. For example, you might say, "I went to the beach, but then it started to snow." Next, another player might add to the problem by saying, "The snow turned to ice." Then, another player might make the problem even crazier by saying, "The ice formed a big ice mountain." Make the story as crazy as you can. Then, work together to draw all the problems in the story. (If you want to start out with a well-known story, try it with "The old lady who swallowed a fly.")

Using Your Head

{ **10** }
minutes

*Grab a **pencil**!*

Reread "Race Against the Rain" on page 108. The family went camping, but then it was going to rain. Look for ways that the family dealt with this problem. Then, write the ways they solved the problem on each line below.

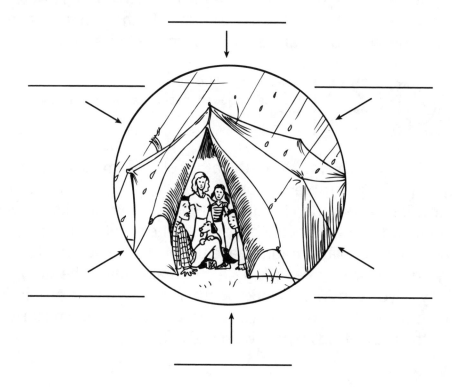

Answers: Paul put away lunch. Paul checked for warm clothes. Paul got flashlights and a lantern. Zelda raked pine needles. Everyone put the tent together. Doodad reminded everyone about the rain.

Comparing and Contrasting

Say two friends are eating dessert. One friend loves ice cream for dessert, but the other friend loves brownies for dessert. A third grader might be able to say that the two friends are different because they like different kinds of desserts. But, given the same information, could your kid notice how the two friends are alike? Perhaps after thinking about it, your kid might realize that both friends are eating dessert and love sweets!

Many third graders can often identify things that are obviously alike and different in their reading. However, facing longer and more complex texts, kids may have a tough time sorting out which similarities and differences are important within the context of a story. Your kid needs to practice working with obvious and subtle similarities and differences.

First things first: Get a sense of what your kid already knows. Turn the page and tell your kid to Jump Right In!

Here's what you'll need for this lesson:
- *pencil*
- *paper*
- *magazines, newspapers, or catalogs*
- *alarm clock or timer*

 **Jump Right In!**

Two Explorers

Sue Hendrickson is an American woman who will go anywhere in the world for an adventure. Most of all, she loves to explore the ocean. One of her first jobs was to find tropical fish for pet stores and aquariums. Another job was to dive for beautiful shells on the ocean floor. Now, Sue goes on diving missions to investigate ships and ancient cities that have sunk to the bottom of the sea. One time, Sue worked with a team of divers to learn about a 400-year-old Spanish ship. They found many silver and gold coins and nearly 1,000 Chinese pots. On another mission, Sue went diving in Egypt to explore a sunken city. She found buildings, bridges, coins, vases, and other treasures that were thousands of years old. Sue is able to learn about the way people used to live by studying the things she finds underwater.

Alexandra David-Néel was an explorer of a different kind. She was born in France. Her curiosity about the people and cultures of Asia led her far from home. She traveled to India, Japan, and even to the highest city in the world. That city was Lhasa, the capital of Tibet. Tibet is a small state high in the Himalaya Mountains. These are the tallest mountains in the world. At the time that Alexandra went there, outsiders were not allowed into Lhasa. It was known as a "forbidden" city. It took Alexandra a year to prepare for her trip. She had help from a boy named Yongden. Alexandra and Yongden disguised themselves in order to be allowed to enter Lhasa. When they got into the city, they watched and learned all about the way people lived in Lhasa. After staying for two months, Alexandra returned to France and wrote a book about her adventure.

1. How are Sue and Alexandra alike?

   A. They both traveled to other countries.

   B. They both went to "forbidden" cities.

   C. They both were born in France.

   D. They both climbed the Himalayas.

2. How are Sue and Alexandra different?

   A. Alexandra prefers to explore the ocean.

   B. Alexandra had to wear a disguise.

   C. Sue likes to go on adventures alone.

   D. Sue never climbs mountains.

3. What is one important way that Sue and Alexandra are alike?

   _____

   _____

4. What is one important difference between Sue and Alexandra?

   _____

   _____

Excellent Job!

 **Checking In**

Answers for page 117:

1. A

2. B

3. An A+ answer: "Sue and Alexandra are both curious and explore faraway places to learn about other people and cultures."

4. An A+ answer: "Sue learns about people by investigating ancient cities and ships, and Alexandra watched the way people live to learn more about them."

Did your child get the answers correct? If so, ask your child to point out any other similarities and differences. For example, your child might say that Sue and Alexandra are both women and both work hard. Your child might also say that Sue is an American, whereas Alexandra is French.

Did your child get any of the answers wrong? Sometimes third graders have difficulty making sense of lots of details. Help your child organize all the details. Ask your child to write a list of descriptions about Sue on the left side of a piece of paper and then write a list of descriptions about Alexandra on the right side. Then, ask your child to circle all the similarities and underline all the differences. Talk through any instances when your child is confused.

 **Watch Out!**

Kids sometimes have to use the details directly stated to develop a more subtle sense of a character or story. For example, with question 2, your child might have mistakenly decided that Sue never climbs mountains because she usually explores the ocean. Show your child that the passage also says that Sue will go anywhere for an adventure. Explain to your child that the passage never says she won't climb a mountain and that this detail means that she might go to a mountain for an adventure.

What to Know...

By taking in the details in a story, your kid can identify similarities and differences. Your kid might start to use the words *alike* and *different* with confidence. By doing this, your kid gains a deeper understanding of characters, events, and purpose in different stories.

Review these skills with your child this way:

- **Comparing** is noting what is alike between two or more ideas, characters, details, or events in a passage. Your kid says things are "alike."

- **Contrasting** is noting what is different between two or more ideas, characters, details, or events in a passage. Your kid says things are "different."

Sometimes your kid has to think past the details provided to figure out how things are alike or different.

> After school, Mary and Joey eat snacks. Mary likes apples. Joey likes soup.

> The museum has a room full of pottery from China. Some of the pottery is new, and some is very old.

> Lara and Jose went to the park. Lara played on the swing set, and Jose played basketball.

For each paragraph, ask your child to identify how the characters, details, or events are alike and how they are different.

On Your Way to an "A" Activities

20 minutes

Type: Active
Materials needed: none
Number of players: 5 or more

Players take turns being "It." The player who is "It" stands. The other players sit in a circle around "It." "It" should carefully study all the details of the room and the other players, and then leave the room. Then, the group changes one thing. For example, all the players could take off their shoes. Then, "It" returns and has to guess the change. As soon as "It" guesses correctly, another player can be "It."

15 minutes

Type: Game/Competitive
Materials needed: magazines, newspapers, catalogs, pencils, paper, timer or alarm clock
Number of players: 2 or more

Find 2 pictures in a magazine, newspaper, or catalog. Set a timer or alarm clock to go off after 5 minutes. During this time, each player writes a list of things that are alike or different in both pictures. After 5 minutes, the players share what they found to be alike. For each thing a player finds that no one else finds, the player gets a point. Then, the players share what they found to be different. For each thing a player finds that no one else finds, the player gets a point. The player with the most points wins the round. Play another round by using 2 new pictures.

Using Your Head

*Grab a **pencil**!*

Reread the first paragraph of "Two Explorers." Then, read the poem below and complete the exercise on the next page.

The Find

Wandering the beach one afternoon
I come upon a tide pool—
A bowl of seaweed-covered rocks
Filled with high tide water that got left behind.

All is still as I look in.
No fish, I think, too bad, now what?
And then, a shimmer,
But not the scaly gleam of a silvery fish.
It's a golden glint, winking at me from under water.

I close my fist around the shiny thing.
It's round and smooth and heavy in my hand.
I bring it up into the light, unwrap my fingers, and see
A gold coin, old, old, old, big, lumpy, worn down by the sea.

When I gaze back into the tide pool,
I see another coin, another, and another!
It occurs to me to wonder then
What person, way back long ago
Came to leave this pile of coins here by the sea?

In the left-hand circle, write details from the story about Sue on page 116 that are different from the details in this poem. In the right-hand circle, write details from the poem that are different from the details in the story about Sue. In the part where the circles overlap, write details that are alike.

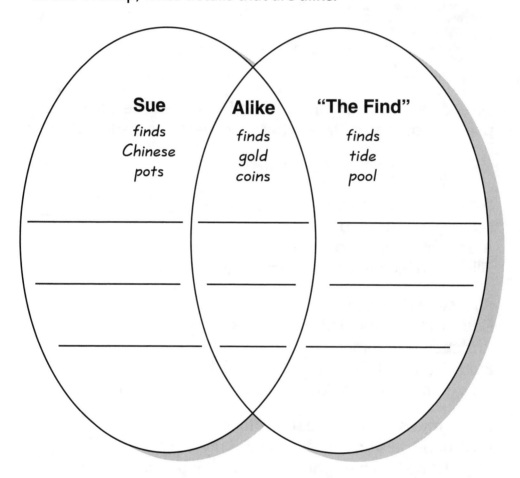

Sue

finds Chinese pots

Alike

finds gold coins

"The Find"

finds tide pool

Cause and Effect

Chances are your child is good at identifying obvious causes and effects. If your child sees a movie in which a bathtub faucet is turned on, your kid knows that the bathtub filling with water is a *result*.

But sometimes your kid doesn't realize less obvious causes and effects. What if the next scene in the movie shows a flooded living room? One cause might be that no one turned off the bathtub faucet. A related cause might be that the person who turned it on fell asleep, was kidnapped, or simply forgot. Movies constantly jump from scene to scene and expect audiences to make the cause-and-effect relationships based just on what they see.

As your kid grows up, cause-and-effect relationships may seem less and less obvious. If your kid ever broke something, played football in the living room, or tried to jump off a tall object, you may have asked your kid, "What were you thinking?" You know your kid can sometimes get carried away by an idea without realizing the consequences—especially when those consequences aren't blatantly obvious.

So, now that your kid is reading longer and more complicated stories, she's reading about more and more cases in which neither the cause nor the consequence are so obvious. It's time for her to develop her ability to recognize and connect these more subtle cause-and-effect relationships.

First things first: Get a sense of what your kid already knows. Turn the page and tell your kid to Jump Right In!

Here's what you'll need for this lesson:
- *pencils*
- *paper*
- *a current newspaper*
- *red, blue, and yellow food coloring*
- *three clear glasses of water*

 **Jump Right In!**

The Time Capsule

Everyone was getting ready for this year's school fair. Leo was writing a play. Darrell was making costumes for Leo's play. Kendra and Matt were planning a "How Many Jelly Beans Are in the Jar?" contest.

Gino wanted to do something special for the fair. He hoped he might get ideas for the fair, but he couldn't think of anything. So, he went to the library. He read about fairs held at other schools. "I've got it!" he exclaimed suddenly. Everyone in the library looked up from their books.

Gino decided he would make a time capsule. "A time capsule holds things from our lives. The time capsule gets put underground. Then, in 100 years, people can open it up. They can learn what it was like to be us!"

Gino set to work. First he talked to classmates, parents, and teachers. He asked them what things should go into the capsule. Gino remembered that his uncle had an old metal trunk in his garage. His uncle didn't use it. It was gathering dust. So, Gino asked his uncle if he could have it. Next, Gino asked the school custodian for help. They picked a good place to bury the time capsule. Then, they dug a deep hole under a tree in the school yard.

Gino collected things to put in the trunk, but waited. On the day of the fair, Gino held a ceremony. He showed the crowd the things he picked out. Then, he carefully closed the trunk. Finally, the custodian lowered the trunk into the deep hole. Gino covered it up. He hoped people living in 100 years would be interested in learning about his time capsule.

1. Gino went to the library because

   A. the school custodian was there

   B. Darrell left a book about costumes in the library

   C. he wanted to put a book in his time capsule

   D. he wanted to get ideas for the fair

2. Gino held a ceremony during the fair

   A. to give awards for the best project at the school fair

   B. to read books about school fairs to everyone in the crowd

   C. to show people what he was putting in the time capsule

   D. so everyone would help dig a hole

3. What effect did Gino want the time capsule to have on people in the future?

_____

_____

_____

Excellent Job!

 **Checking In**

Answers for page 125:

1. D

2. C

3. An A+ answer: "He wanted the things in the time capsule to help people 100 years from now understand what our lives are like today."

Did your child get the answers correct? If so, review question 1. Ask your child to identify the *cause* and the *effect*. You could ask, "Is Gino going to the library the *cause* or the *effect*?" Do the same for question 2.

Did your child get any of the answers wrong? If so, your child might be having a hard time reading the long answer choices. Encourage your child to mark whether each answer choice could be wrong or right. For example, read all the answer choices to question 2. Tell your child to draw a check mark next to answer choices that could be right and to draw a line through the letter of answer choices that are probably wrong. Then, ask your child to pick the correct answer from the choices with check marks.

 **Watch Out!**

Kids are used to focusing on the events in stories, but they may be unfamiliar with understanding the relationships between events. Your kid may need practice making connections between events. Work with your child by pointing out events that are connected in a story and asking, "How did this event cause the other thing to happen?" For example, you could ask, "What caused everyone in the library to look up from their books?"

What to Know...

In most stories your kid reads, a *cause* is related before its *effect*. So, your kid may be used to seeing causes presented before their effects in texts. But this isn't always what happens.

Review these skills with your child this way:

- The **cause** is the reason an event happens.
- The **effect** is the result of an event, feeling, or idea.

Your child needs to see the relationship between events to understand cause and effect.

Story 1: Her kite flew away and got stuck in a tree. Samantha was shocked. Just a few minutes ago, the wind had started to blow a little harder.

Story 2: Samantha felt the wind blow harder. Her kite flew away and got stuck in a tree. Samantha was shocked.

Explain to your child that the cause-and-effect relationships in the two stories are the same. Ask your child to identify the cause-and-effect relationships.

Third Graders Are...

Sometimes third graders can get tangled in complicated details. Help your child boil down cause-and-effect relationships by drawing arrows between separate events in a story that are linked by cause and effect.

On Your Way to an "A" Activities

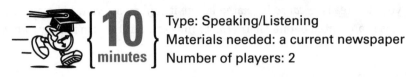

Type: Speaking/Listening
Materials needed: a current newspaper
Number of players: 2

Ask a friend or parent to read you the last part of a newspaper article describing a recent event. Make sure it's not an event that you already know about! Then, try to guess the cause of the event. For example, if the article is about how a court trial came out, guess what crime was committed that led to the trial. If the event describes a celebration, try to guess the reason the celebration was held. Then, have your friend or parent read the beginning of the article, and see how close you came to figuring out its cause.

Study Right

Children this age sometimes speed-read stories to come up with an answer *fast*. Sometimes they guess the first answer that comes to mind without considering all the possibilities. Explain to your kid that he or she needs to know that reading and thinking take time. Work on this by asking your child detailed questions about how something that happened early in a story connects with something that happened later. If your child has trouble linking these events, ask him or her to reread the relevant parts of the story slowly and carefully, and then try answering your question again.

Type: Active
Materials needed: none
Number of players: 3 or more

Play "Freeze Fast!" Each player thinks of an action. One player acts out his or her action and then "freezes," staying absolutely still. A player who thinks of a possible effect of the action taps the frozen player, who then sits down. Then, this other player can act out the effect. Keep going until everyone has acted out an action and an effect of an action. For example, the first player can stretch, yawn, and lay down. Another player can take over this action by pretending to fall asleep. Or a player can pretend to hit a baseball. Another player can show the effect and pretend to be the baseball flying far over a field or the player running around the bases.

Type: Arts and crafts
Materials needed: red, blue, and yellow food coloring; three clear glasses of water; pencil and paper
Number of players: 1 or more

Fill each glass with water. Put 3 drops of red food coloring in one glass, 3 drops of blue food coloring in another glass, and 3 drops of yellow food coloring in the third glass. On a sheet of paper, write down what you think the effect might be when you add a drop of blue food coloring to the red water, what might happen when you add a drop of yellow to the blue water, and what might happen when you add a drop of red to the yellow water.

Now, test the effects you guessed at by carrying out the experiment. Put a drop of blue into the red water, a drop of yellow into the blue, and a drop of red into the yellow water. Did you guess the correct effects of what happens when you mix colors?

Has your child breezed through the activities? If so, he or she can work on this Using Your Head activity independently.

Using Your Head

{ **15** minutes }

*Grab a **pencil**!*

Look at the pictures below. On the left are causes. On the right are effects. Draw a line from each cause to its effect.

Cause

1.

2.

3.

4.

Effect

A.

B.

C.

D.

Fact and Opinion

In third grade, kids are still figuring out their own sense of right and wrong, and sometimes still blending the real with the unreal. As a result, your kid may find it hard to tell facts and opinions apart.

Also, kids at this age can feel confused about what they *know* to be true and what is a fact. For example, your child may have just recently figured out that she really likes tomato sandwiches. She feels so clearly about her love of tomato sandwiches that she may mistakenly think that it's a fact that tomato sandwiches taste great to everyone.

Give your child guidelines for telling the difference between facts and opinions. Your child can do research with dictionaries and the Internet to find out if a statement is a fact. Or your child can conduct mini-surveys around the house and neighborhood. (If your kid asked her neighbors if they liked tomato sandwiches, your child might quickly understand that a preference for tomato sandwiches is an opinion.) In the long run, your child will learn a very important lesson for life—that not all things that sound like facts are facts and that not all opinions are right for everyone.

First things first: Get a sense of what your kid already knows. Turn the page and tell your kid to Jump Right In!

Here's what you'll need for this lesson:
- pencils
- paper
- dictionary
- poster paper
- scissors
- glue
- newspapers, magazines, and/or catalogs
- crayons or markers

 **Jump Right In!**

Show-and-Tell

Kim loved the zoo. She was going to go with her class at school. To prepare, they did a show-and-tell. Students stood in front of the class and shared what they knew about animals and zoos.

Cato volunteered to go first. "Elephants come from Asia and Africa," she said. "They can suck water into their trunks. Then, they can blow the water into their mouths." She held open an encyclopedia with a photograph of an elephant blowing water into its mouth. "An elephant's trunk has 100,000 muscles in it." Cato sat down, and everyone clapped. But Frank wasn't clapping.

"All I know is that all elephants are ugly," said Frank. "I think black bears are much cooler animals than elephants!"

"That's what you think," Cato said. "*I* just happen to think elephants are awesome."

Then it was Frank's turn. He walked to the front of the classroom. "There are eight kinds of bears in the world. Black bears can run as fast as 35 miles per hour!" said Frank.

Cato shook her head. Cato liked elephants more than bears. Kim wasn't sure what animal was her favorite, but she did know what she would talk about in class.

Kim said, "My sister is a zoologist. That means she works at a zoo. Some zoologists like to work with one type of animal the best. Other zoologists care for many different animals." She smiled and sat down.

1. What is an opinion in this story?

   A. There are eight kinds of bears.

   B. Kim's sister is a zoologist.

   C. All elephants are ugly.

   D. Elephants use their trunks.

2. What is a fact in this story?

   A. An elephant's trunk has 100,000 muscles.

   B. Black bears are cooler than elephants.

   C. Elephants from Asia and Africa are beautiful.

   D. Visiting the zoo for school is fun.

3. What is another fact in the story? How do you know this is a fact?

   _____

   _____

4. What is another opinion in the story? How do you know this is an opinion?

   _____

   _____

Excellent Job!

 *Checking In*

Ⓐ Answers for page 133:

1. C

2. A

3. An A+ answer: "Elephants can blow water into their mouths. This is a fact because it can be proven to be true. Also, Cato has an encyclopedia that shows a photograph of an elephant doing this, which proves it's true."

4. An A+ answer: "Elephants are awesome. This is an opinion because it is Cato's belief. Frank doesn't have the same belief. It can't be proven that elephants are awesome."

Did your child get the answers correct? If so, ask your child to share facts she has about zoos and animals. Then, ask your child to share opinions she has about animals. Discuss how all of the facts can or have been proven to be true, whereas the opinions can't be.

Did your child get any of the answers wrong? Facts and opinions aren't always easy to tell apart. Say to your child, "Just because you agree with something doesn't make it a fact. A fact can be proven to be true, and opinions cannot be. Let's talk about each opinion together."

 *Watch Out!*

Opinions sometimes come disguised as facts. In this story, Frank says, "All I know is that all elephants are ugly." Kids might think that because someone says they "know" something, that it's a fact. Talk about what Frank says with your child. Explain that he expresses an opinion because no one could prove that all elephants are ugly—it's a point of view or opinion, not a fact.

What to Know...

Sorting out facts from opinions can be confusing, especially when more than one person holds a strong belief, and as a group they claim that what they believe is the truth. The difference is in the proof.

Review these skills with your child this way:

- **Facts** are statements that are true. Facts can be about people, places, numbers, and many other things.
- **Opinions** are beliefs or judgments held by a person or a group. Opinions may be supported by information, but they cannot be proven to be true.

Read this passage with your child to explore the differences between facts and opinions.

Bianca hates broccoli. Her whole family hates broccoli. They all say that broccoli tastes bad. Her dad says he once saw a piece of broccoli that was pink with black dots and moved.

Then one evening, Bianca has supper at her friend Josie's house. Can you guess what they're having? Broccoli! Raw broccoli salad, broccoli pie, and broccoli soup. Josie's family says that broccoli contains many vitamins and minerals. Josie's mom says that broccoli is a green vegetable grown in many places around the world. Josie's family thinks broccoli tastes great.

· · · · · · · · · · · ● ●

Ask your child to identify the facts and opinions in the passage.

Most kids can identify the following facts:

- Broccoli is green.
- Broccoli is a vegetable.
- Broccoli contains vitamins and minerals.
- Broccoli is grown in many places around the world.

Most kids can identify the following opinions:

- Broccoli tastes bad.
- Broccoli tastes great.

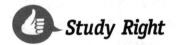 **Study Right**

· · · · · · · · · · · · · · · ●

Ask your child, "How do you know these are facts?" Explain that these could be proven to be true. For example, broccoli is never an animal—it is always a vegetable.

· · · · · · · · · · · · · · ●

Ask your child, "How do you know these are opinions?" Explain that opinions can't be proven. There can always be a different opinion. For example, some might say broccoli tastes bad, but others could say broccoli tastes great. Ask your child to imagine other opinions.

In order to sort fact from opinion, kids need to learn to consult reliable sources of information. Help your child find information by steering him or her to resources such as dictionaries, encyclopedias, or reliable Web sites on the Internet. Consulting these resources will not only help your child differentiate fact from opinion, but will encourage a curiosity about the world.

Third Graders Are...

At this age, children are still developing their sense of the world beyond themselves. They may not recognize that something they "know" to be true is actually an opinion and not a fact. For example, if your child doesn't like broccoli, he or she may feel that Bianca's family is saying facts, when they are actually sharing opinions. Encourage your child to check what he or she "knows" against reliable outside sources.

On Your Way to an "A" Activities

10 minutes

Type: Game/Competitive
Materials needed: a dictionary, pencils, paper
Number of players: 3 or more

One player picks a word from the dictionary. It has to be a word no one knows. The player reads the word aloud. Then, this player reads five different definitions from the dictionary—one of the definitions should be the definition of the word. The other four definitions should be the definitions of other words. The other players each guess which definition is the real definition. See how easy or hard it is to know the real definition. The players that guess correctly get a point. Then, another player can take a turn with the dictionary. The player with the most points wins.

20 minutes

Type: Arts and Crafts
Materials needed: poster paper, scissors, glue, newspapers, magazines, catalogs, pencils, crayons or markers
Number of players: 1 or more

Make a fact collage and an opinion collage. Go through the newspaper, magazines, and catalogs and cut out pictures or sentences that express facts or opinions. Glue the facts to one piece of paper and the opinions to the other.

Using Your Head

{ **15** minutes }

*Grab a **pencil**!*

Read the sentence next to each picture. Then, write "F" if it's a fact or "O" if it's an opinion.

1. Zebras have black and white stripes.

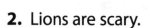

2. Lions are scary.

3. Pandas eat bamboo.

4. Gorillas look a little like people.

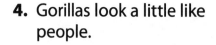

Answers: 1. F; 2. O; 3. F; 4. O

Addition and Subtraction

By the time your kid is in third grade, he or she might feel like an old pro at adding and subtracting basic facts. But third-grade mathematics requires the mastery of adding and subtracting larger numbers. This type of addition and subtraction involves numbers too large to count very easily. Your child may suddenly find that adding and subtracting is confusing again.

In the last few years, while your child was learning basic addition and subtraction facts, he or she was probably also learning about place value. Now, your child needs to apply what he or she knows about place value to regrouping (also known as "borrowing" or "carrying"). Once your child gets the hang of this, adding and subtracting with larger numbers may seem like old hat.

First things first: Get a sense of what your kid already knows. Turn the page and tell your kid to Jump Right In!

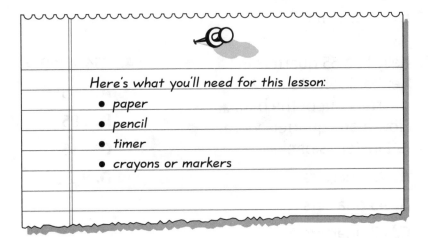

Here's what you'll need for this lesson:
- *paper*
- *pencil*
- *timer*
- *crayons or markers*

Jump Right In!

1. Last week, Jack scored 256 points playing his favorite video game. This week, he has scored 88 points. How many points has Jack scored so far?

   A. 232 points

   B. 234 points

   C. 334 points

   D. 344 points

2. Kelly had 55 quarters in her bank. She took 12 quarters out of the bank. How many quarters were left in Kelly's bank?

   A. 42 quarters

   B. 43 quarters

   C. 67 quarters

   D. 77 quarters

3.   26
     + 3
   ———

   A. 23

   B. 25

   C. 29

   D. 31

4. 754 − 469 =

   A. 185

   B. 285

   C. 315

   D. 1,223

Excellent Job!

Cracking the Third Grade

 *Checking In*

❶ Answers for page 142:

    1. D

    2. B

    3. C

    4. B

Did your child get the correct answers? If so, ask, "When the sum of the digits in a certain place value is 10 or more, what do you do?" You can also ask, "Can you explain to me how to regroup when subtracting?"

Did your child get any of the answers wrong? If so, ask your to child explain the steps he or she took to answer the questions. Find out if your child has difficulty adding, subtracting, adding with regrouping, and/or subtracting with regrouping. If your child answered questions 2 and 3 incorrectly, then review basic addition and subtraction facts. If your child answered questions 1 and 4 incorrectly, review how to regroup (10 ones = 1 ten, 10 tens = 1 hundred).

 *Watch Out!*

Sometimes third graders make mistakes when writing their problems. For example, with questions 1, 2, and 4, your child has to write the numbers, lined up by place value. For example, in question 1, students are required to add 256 and 88.

Your child's work should look like $\begin{array}{r} 256 \\ + 88 \\ \hline \end{array}$, but your child might have incorrectly written the problem as $\begin{array}{r} 256 \\ + 88 \\ \hline \end{array}$ or $\begin{array}{r} 256 \\ + 88 \\ \hline \end{array}$. Make sure your child knows to line up the digits by place value, with the ones in the same column, the tens in the same column, and so on, before adding or subtracting.

What to Know...

Your child is learning to regroup when adding and subtracting. "Regrouping" is what educators now call the skills you might have called "carrying" and "borrowing."

Review these skills with your child this way:

- **Addition** is an operation that combines numbers.

- The **sum** is a number that results from adding numbers.

- **Subtraction** is an operation on two numbers that tells the difference between the numbers.

- The **difference** is a number that results from subtracting a number from another number.

Your child might use these skills when adding packets of flower seeds.

Explain that 7 ones + 6 ones = 13 ones, or 1 ten and 3 ones. Your child should write 1 above the tens column and 3 in the ones place of the answer. Then, add the tens and re-group (1 ten + 2 tens + 8 tens = 11 tens, or 1 hundred and 1 ten). Your child should write a 1 above the hundreds place and a 1 in the tens place of the answer. Ask your child how to finish the rest of the problem.

Your child might subtract seeds already planted from the total number of seeds.

Make sure your child knows that 4 ones cannot be subtracted from 2 ones without regrouping. Explain that 2 tens can be regrouped as 1 ten and 10 ones. So, your child should cross out the 2 tens and write a 1 above it to show the 1 ten. Then, your child can add the 10 ones and the 2 ones to get 12 ones and write 12 in the ones place.

On Your Way to an "A" Activities

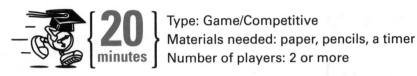

20 minutes

Type: Game/Competitive
Materials needed: paper, pencils, a timer
Number of players: 2 or more

Play "Shop 'til You Drop." Set the timer for 2 minutes. Go around your house and find things you could pretend to buy. Write a list. For example, you might find 12 eggs, 22 cans of food, and 1 basketball. The other players should do the same. When the timer rings, stop finding things to buy. Then, add the numbers of items on your list. Whoever has the most items to buy wins. Play again.

15 minutes

Type: Speaking/Listening
Materials needed: paper and pencils
Number of players: 2 or more

Play a game of "Simon Says Subtraction Regrouping!" One player should be "Simon." Simon says a subtraction problem. Then, Simon says "regroup" or "don't regroup" and stands in a funny way. Simon can try to trick people and say "regroup" when you don't have to regroup or say "don't regroup" when you do have to regroup. The other players write down the numbers and decide if they need to regroup. If they agree with what Simon says, they stand just like Simon. If not, they don't. Players who identified correctly whether they have to regroup or not get to play again.

For example, Simon could say "52 minus 14. Regroup," and stand in a funny way. Then, players who decided they would need to regroup to subtract 14 from 52 would also stand that way, and players who disagree would not. When subtracting 14 from 52, you do need to regroup. Those players who correctly knew to regroup could play again.

Has your child breezed through the activities? If so, he or she can work on this Using Your Head activity independently.

Using Your Head

{ **10** minutes }

*Grab a **pencil** and some **crayons** or **markers**!*

Read each problem. Decide if you have to add or subtract. Circle the word *Add* or *Subtract* to show what you need to do. Then, solve the problem.

1. Jason has 345 baseball cards in his collection. Morgan has 289 baseball cards. How many more cards does Jason have?

   Add   Subtract

2. Kevin had 450 baseball cards. Then, his aunt gave him 34 more cards. How many cards does he have in all?

   Add   Subtract

3. Megan scored 112 points last season. This season she scored 132 points. How many points did she score in all?

   Add   Subtract

Multiplication

Learning to multiply lets your kid become a speed demon. No longer does he or she have to count everything. No longer does he or she have to add many numbers in a row. Your kid can now play and work with numbers more quickly than ever before.

If your kid is feeling thrilled with this new power, that's terrific! But right now, your child is just beginning to learn multiplication and is likely to make a few mistakes. That's okay. Mastering multiplication involves rote memorization of multiplication facts, which might be challenging. However, remind your kid that he or she has already mastered addition and subtraction facts. Mastering multiplication also involves understanding it. Make sure your kid gets all the practice and tools he or she needs both to really understand multiplication and to correctly remember multiplication facts.

First things first: Get a sense of what your kid already knows. Turn the page and tell your kid to Jump Right In!

Here's what you'll need for this lesson:
- *paper*
- *pencil*
- *pennies, dimes, and dollars*
- *scissors*
- *markers or crayons*

Jump Right In!

1. $3 \times 4 =$

    A. 1

    B. 7

    C. 9

    D. 12

2. $9 \times 2 =$

    A. 7

    B. 11

    C. 18

    D. 27

3. $6 \times 0 =$

    A. 0

    B. 5

    C. 6

    D. 60

4. $1 \times 5 =$

    A. 1

    B. 5

    C. 6

    D. 11

Maria and Jon went to the pond. They got bugs and fish from the pond for science class.

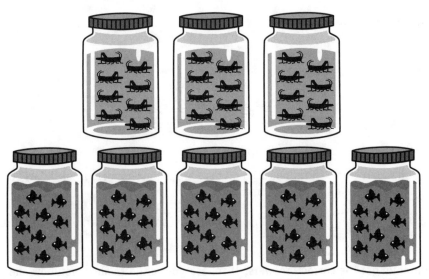

5. Maria got jars of grasshoppers.

How many jars of grasshoppers does she have? _____

How many grasshoppers are in each jar? _____

How many grasshoppers does she have in all?

_____ × _____ = _____

6. Jon got jars of fish.

How many jars of fish does he have? _____

How many fish are in each jar? _____

How many fish does he have in all?

_____ × _____ = _____

ⓐAnswers for pages 148 and 149:

1. D

2. C

3. A

4. B

5. An A+ answer: "Maria has 3 jars. There are 8 grasshoppers in each jar. So, Maria has 24 grasshoppers in all. $3 \times 8 = 24$."

6. An A+ answer: "Jon has 5 jars. There are 10 fish in each jar. So, Jon has 50 fish in all. $5 \times 10 = 50$."

Did your child get the correct answers? If so, ask your child to show you how she answered one of the questions. Make sure your child can find the correct answer again.

Did your child get any of the answers wrong? Find out if your child knew to multiply but made an error. If so, explain that he can check his answers by using repeated addition. For question 1, your child might not know for sure if $3 \times 4 = 12$, so he can check his answer by adding 3 four times ($3 + 3 + 3 + 3 = 12$).

 *Watch Out!*

Sometimes third graders mix up addition, subtraction, and multiplication. Write down the addition sign (+) and say that this means to add, the subtraction sign (–) and say that this means to subtract, and the multiplication sign (×) and say that this means to multiply.

Then, have your kid flip through this book, identify signs, and give an example of how each could be used. So, if your kid finds an addition sign (+), he or she might say, "This is an addition sign or a plus sign. $2 + 5 = 7$" or "This is a multiplication sign (×). $2 \times 5 = 10$."

What to Know...

Kids can use multiplication to figure out things quickly, such as, "How many fireflies do I have?"

Review these skills with your child this way:

- **Equal groups** are groups that all have the same number of objects.
- **Multiplication** is an operation that combines equal groups to find a result. (One way to combine equal groups is through repeated addition.)
- The **multiplication sign** is ×. When your child sees ×, he or she can say "times."
- A **factor** is a number multiplied by another number.
- A **product** is a number that is the result of multiplying numbers.

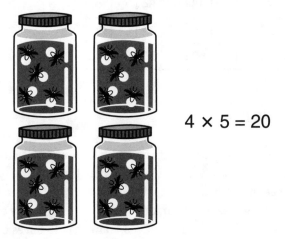

$$4 \times 5 = 20$$

Ask your child to count all the fireflies in each jar. Explain that there are 5 fireflies in each jar, so these are equal groups of fireflies. Then, ask your child to identify the factors (4 and 5) and the product (20).

 **Checking In**

Does your child struggle to grasp the concept of multiplication? Help by showing equal groups. Use something that your child is familiar with, such as buttons, toys, socks, or other everyday objects. Make different collections of equal groups (5 groups of 4 socks, 9 groups of 7 checkers, etc.). Have your child count the objects and figure out that there are equal groups. Then, ask your child to use multiplication to find the total number of objects.

Your child can use basic multiplication facts.

×	0	1	2	3	4	5	6	7	8	9	10
0	0	0	0	0	0	0	0	0	0	0	0
1	0	1	2	3	4	5	6	7	8	9	10
2	0	2	4	6	8	10	12	14	16	18	20
3	0	3	6	9	12	15	18	21	24	27	30
4	0	4	8	12	16	20	24	28	32	36	40
5	0	5	10	15	20	25	30	35	40	45	50
6	0	6	12	18	24	30	36	42	48	54	60
7	0	7	14	21	28	35	42	49	56	63	70
8	0	8	16	24	32	40	48	56	64	72	80
9	0	9	18	27	36	45	54	63	72	81	90
10	0	10	20	30	40	50	60	70	80	90	100

Ask your child to say the multiplication facts aloud. Ask your child to review his work from pages 148 and 149 using these multiplication facts.

 Watch Out!

Third graders often get multiplication facts involving 0, 1, and 10 confused. Help them by pointing out when these facts are useful in everyday life. For example, facts involving 10 are useful when dealing with money because our money system is a base-ten system. Use dollars, dimes, and pennies. Ask your kid to figure out how many dimes are equal to 1 dollar, 2 dollars, 3 dollars, and so on. Say, "You know that 10 dimes equal 1 dollar, and 1 times 10 equals 10. So, you can use multiplication to figure out that there are 10 dimes in 1 dollar." Or say, "Imagine you want to trade 4 dollars for dimes. You know that there are 10 dimes in 1 dollar, and 4 times 10 equals 40. So, there are 40 dimes in 4 dollars." Do the same with exchanging pennies for dimes.

Third Graders Are...

Third graders are eager to perform new mathematics skills and enjoy regular practice. So, feel free to keep reviewing the multiplication facts as often as your kid wants to. You can have your kid turn them into songs, draw them as pictures, or use them every day during errands and tasks.

On Your Way to an "A" Activities

15 minutes

Type: Game/Competitive
Materials needed: paper, pencil, pennies
Number of players: 3 or more

Play "Bingo." One player has to be the caller. The other players should draw five-by-five grids on paper. Each player should write a different multiplication fact in each square of his or her grid (like $4 \times 3 = 12$). The caller calls out a multiplication fact. Check to see if you have this fact correctly on your card. If you do, cover the fact with a penny. The first player to cover five facts in a row across, down, up, or diagonally wins.

20 minutes

Type: Active
Materials needed: dollars, dimes, and pennies (or paper, crayons, and scissors to make fake money)
Number of players: 2 or more

Play "Bank." Pretend that you have a bank. One player should be the banker and run the bank. The other player comes into the bank with money that he or she needs to change. For example, this player could have 10 pennies and want dimes. The banker decides how much the player's money is worth. Take turns.

Has your child breezed through the activities? If so, he or she can work on this Using Your Head activity independently.

Using Your Head

{ **15** minutes }

*Grab a **pencil** and some **crayons** or **markers**!*

For each multiplication fact, draw equal groups of bugs or fish. Then, find the product.

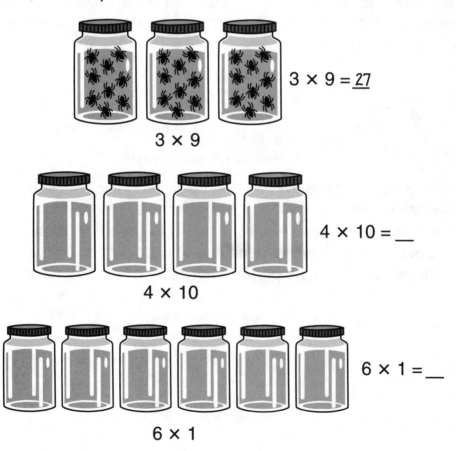

$3 \times 9 = \underline{27}$

3×9

$4 \times 10 = \underline{}$

4×10

$6 \times 1 = \underline{}$

6×1

Answers: 3 jars with 9 spiders = 27 spiders; 4 jars with 10 bugs/fish in each jar = 40; 6 jars with 1 bug/fish in each jar = 6

Cracking the Third Grade

Division

Your kid probably has a lot of experience sharing—toys, food, chores, TV time. Whenever you've told your kid, "Be fair and share equally," you've been getting her to divide.

Now your child is beginning to learn formal rules of division. Chances are that he's starting to use division in math class. He also may be asked to answer division problems involving only numbers, not objects or pictures. Faced with these abstract problems, your kid might get lost. He needs to relate the new rules he is learning to what he already knows about division.

When it comes to receiving a shared amount of food or toys, children are highly motivated—they want to make sure they received their fair share. This should get your kid geared up to learn division and memorize division facts.

First things first: Get a sense of what your kid already knows. Turn the page and tell your kid to Jump Right In!

Here's what you'll need for this lesson:
- *pencil*
- *16 index cards*
- *crayons or markers*
- *chalk*
- *pebble*

1. $15 \div 3 =$

    A. 3

    B. 5

    C. 12

    D. 45

2. $8 \div 4 =$

    A. 2

    B. 4

    C. 10

    D. 16

3. Which one of these shows $12 \div 3$?

A.

B.

C.

D.

Linda has $20. She wants to buy gifts for friends.

Gifts for Friends

	Books	$5
	CDs	$10
	Notebooks	$1

4. Linda thinks she might buy only books. How many books can she buy?

$20 ÷ _____ = _____

5. Linda thinks she might buy only CDs. How many CDs can she buy?

$20 ÷ _____ = _____

6. Linda thinks she might buy only notebooks. How many notebooks can she buy?

$20 ÷ _____ = _____

Excellent Job!

 **Checking In**

Ⓐ Answers for pages 156 and 157:

1. B

2. A

3. B

4. An A+ answer: "$20 ÷ $5 = 4 books. Linda can buy 4 books."

5. An A+ answer: "$20 ÷ $10 = 2 CDs. Linda can buy 2 CDs."

6. An A+ answer: "$20 ÷ $1 = 20 notebooks. Linda can buy 20 notebooks."

Did your child get the correct answers? If so, ask your child to draw a picture showing the division facts and labeling the picture.

Did your child get any of the answers wrong? If so, tell your child to use what he knows about multiplication to answer division problems. Use groups of pennies to show your child that 3 equal groups of 4 pennies means there is a total of 12 pennies. Then, show your child how 12 pennies divides into 3 equal groups of 4 pennies. For question 2, ask your child, "4 times what equals 8?"

 **Watch Out!**

Sometimes third graders see two numbers in a problem and just guess at what they should do. They add, subtract, multiply, or divide without any thought to why they are doing something. Go over different problems from lessons 1, 2, and 3. Ask your child to figure out how to solve each problem. Tell your child to draw a picture of what the problem is describing to help figure out how to solve it.

What to Know...

Kids use division all the time when they are sharing. Review these skills with your child this way:

- **Equal groups** are groups that have the same number of items in them.

- **Division** is an operation with two numbers that tells how many groups there are. It also tells how many items are in each group. The **division sign** is ÷.

- The **quotient** is a number resulting from dividing a number by another number. For example, in 24 ÷ 8 = 3, the quotient is 3.

Your child could evenly divide a plate of cookies to find out the number of cookies he or she could give to friends.

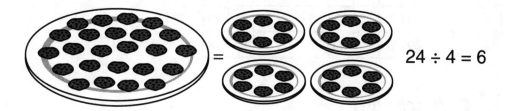

Ask your child to count all the cookies on the big plate. Then, ask your child to count the number of small plates. Explain how this shows that there are 24 cookies being divided by 4. Next, ask your child to count the number of cookies on each small plate. Explain that there are 6 cookies on each small plate, so these are equal groups. Then, ask your child to identify the quotient (6).

Your child can use basic division facts.

×/÷	0	1	2	3	4	5	6	7	8	9	10
0	0	0	0	0	0	0	0	0	0	0	0
1	0	1	2	3	4	5	6	7	8	9	10
2	0	2	4	6	8	10	12	14	16	18	20
3	0	3	6	9	12	15	18	21	24	27	30
4	0	4	8	12	16	20	24	28	32	36	40
5	0	5	10	15	20	25	30	35	40	45	50
6	0	6	12	18	24	30	36	42	48	54	60
7	0	7	14	21	28	35	42	49	56	63	70
8	0	8	16	24	32	40	48	56	64	72	80
9	0	9	18	27	36	45	54	63	72	81	90
10	0	10	20	30	40	50	60	70	80	90	100

Ask your child to say the division facts aloud. Ask your child to review her work from pages 156 and 157 using these division facts.

 Watch Out!

Does your child remember all of these division facts? If not, find out what facts your child remembers and what facts your child forgets. Often, kids will be really good at some facts and totally forget another set of facts. Go over the facts your kid forgets.

 Study Right

Make flash cards for multiplication facts and division facts. Making flash cards is a great skill to learn at this age, and it is one that will be used throughout your child's school career.

Third Graders Are...

Most third graders are just starting to hit the developmental period when they can begin to think abstractly. Division is an abstract concept. Some third graders may not yet be ready, however. Every child grows at his or her own pace. Having your kid use division in everyday life can make the abstract concept of division more concrete.

On Your Way to an "A" Activities

25 minutes

Type: Game/Competitive
Materials needed: 16 index cards, crayons or markers
Number of players: 2

Write a different division problem (but not the answer) on each of 8 index cards. Make sure each problem has a different answer. Write the answers to the division problems on 8 separate index cards. Shuffle the cards. Then, lay them out facedown in four rows of four cards. Take turns picking two cards. If you pick a division problem and its correct answer, then keep that pair. If you don't, put them back facedown. Whoever has the most pairs at the end wins!

15 minutes

Type: Active
Materials needed: chalk and a pebble
Number of players: 2 or more

Draw a long hopscotch playing area on a safe sidewalk. Use different shapes and make sure the shapes connect. Write a different division problem in each shape (but not the answer). Then, throw a pebble into a shape. Say the answer to the division problem, then hop on one foot to that shape. Take turns. If you don't know the answer, you have to skip your turn. Whoever gets the farthest wins.

Has your child breezed through the activities? If so, he or she can work on this Using Your Head activity independently.

Using Your Head

*Grab a **pencil** and some **crayons** or **markers**!*

Divide the food into equal groups. Draw and color the equal groups of food. Then, solve the division problem.

$6 \div 3 =$ __

$15 \div 5 =$ __

$12 \div 4 =$ __

Fractions

How comfortable with fractions is your kid? Most likely, fractions are a new concept. That could be exciting or overwhelming. While multiplication and division required some abstract thought, thinking about values between 0 and 1 can seem like science fiction to your kid.

Many kids have an "ugh" response to fractions. You may have even scowled at your fraction homework as a child. If your kid has a replica of the scowl you had years ago, consider how your own history might inadvertently influence your child's attitude. If fractions were your archenemy, now's the time to look at fractions with clear eyes and a new perspective. Fractions are used all the time—in cooking and measuring, at home, and on the job. If you loved fractions, then let your enthusiasm show. Share your learning experiences. Your kid will feed off them and grow.

It's natural to feel both excited and overwhelmed by learning. Make sure your child understands that these feelings are all part of the process of being a successful learner.

First things first: Get a sense of what your kid already knows. Turn the page and tell your kid to Jump Right In!

Here's what you'll need for this lesson:
- *graph paper or grid paper*
- *pencils*
- *crayons or markers*
- *20 index cards*
- *timer*

1. Which cake is $\frac{1}{4}$ pink?

 **A.**

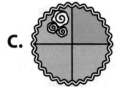 **C.**

 **B.**

 **D.**

2. What fraction of the marbles is black?

A. $\frac{5}{12}$ **C.** $\frac{7}{12}$

B. $\frac{5}{7}$ **D.** $\frac{7}{5}$

3. Which of these shows "two-sixths"?

A. $\dfrac{1}{6}$

C. $2\dfrac{1}{6}$

B. $\dfrac{2}{6}$

D. $\dfrac{26}{6}$

Sammy was playing with a puzzle. Use the picture below to answer questions 4 and 5.

4. Sammy has 7 pieces left to put in the puzzle. What fraction of these leftover pieces is red?

_____

5. What fraction of these leftover pieces is white?

_____

Excellent Job!

 *Checking In*

Answers for pages 164 and 165:

1. C

2. C

3. B

4. An A+ answer: "$\frac{4}{7}$ of the pieces are red."

5. An A+ answer: "$\frac{3}{7}$ of the pieces are white."

Did your child get the correct answers? If so, ask, "How do we use fractions around the house?" Then, ask your child to identify fractions with ordinary objects, such as the number of red pieces in a toy out of the total number of pieces, or the number of cookies eaten out of the total number of cookies.

If your child got any of the answers wrong, go over these answers. Make sure your child knows what number to put in the numerator and what number to put in the denominator. For example, with question 2, your child should count the number of black marbles and put this in the numerator (above the line). Then, your child should count the total number of marbles (black and white) and put this in the denominator (below the line).

Third Graders Are...

Sometimes third graders get excited and rush through their work. Along the way, they might make some mistakes. Encourage your child to take a moment or two to relax after completing the Jump Right In! section. Then, she can check her work with a fresh focus.

What to Know...

Your kid might be used to using division when thinking about sharing (food, games, TV time, etc.). But your kid can also use fractions when sharing.

Review these skills with your child this way:

- A **fraction** is a number that shows part of a group or part of a whole.

- A **numerator** is the number in a fraction that is above the line. The numerator tells how many parts of the whole are being counted.

- A **denominator** is the number in a fraction below the line. The denominator tells how many equal parts are in the whole.

Your child may need to identify fractions for parts of a whole, such as a whole cake, or parts of a group, such as a group of candy.

 $\dfrac{1}{8}$ ←Numerator ←Denominator

· · · · · · · · · · · · ·
Ask your child to count the number of slices that are pink (1) and the number of total slices (8). Then, ask your child to identify the numerator and denominator in the fraction.

 $\dfrac{1}{7}$ ←Numerator ←Denominator

· · · · · · · · · · · · ·
Ask your child to count the number of pieces of candy that are pink (1) and the number of total pieces of candy (7). Then, ask your child to identify the numerator and denominator in the fraction.

Fractions aren't as foreign as they might seem. Whenever your kid uses a ruler, he or she is identifying fractions and mixed numbers on a number line.

Review these skills with your child this way:

- **Whole numbers** are numbers including zero and the counting numbers (0, 1, 2, 3, 4, ...).

- A **mixed number** has a whole number part and a fraction part.

$1\frac{1}{8}$

· · · · · · · · · · · · · •
Point out that 1 whole cake is pink. Then, ask your child to count the number of slices that are pink in the second cake (1) and the number of total slices in the second cake (8). Then, ask your child to identify the whole number and the fraction together.

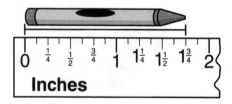

· · · · · · · · · · · •
Ask your child to identify the length of the crayon.

On Your Way to an "A" Activities

15 minutes

Type: Arts and Crafts
Materials needed: graph paper or grid paper, pencils, crayons or markers
Number of players: 1 or more

Make "Fraction Meteors!" Imagine meteors are burning up in space. Draw a meteor on the grid paper that is made up of 4 squares. Then, draw meteors made up of 8, 12, 16, and 20 squares. Imagine that after burning up, only $\frac{1}{4}$ of each meteor is left. Color in $\frac{1}{4}$ of each meteor.

20 minutes

Type: Game/Competitive
Materials needed: 20 index cards, pencils, a timer, crayons or markers
Number of players: 2 or more

Play "Fraction Scavenger Hunt." Write each of these fractions on a different index card: $\frac{1}{6}, \frac{1}{5}, \frac{1}{4}, \frac{1}{3}, \frac{2}{5}, \frac{1}{2}, \frac{3}{5}, \frac{3}{4}$, and $\frac{4}{5}$. Then, shuffle the cards. Every player should pick a card. Don't show the cards to each other. Turn the timer to 5 minutes. Each player should look for his or her fraction around the house, in books, in signs, on boxes or cans of food, and in other places. Each time players find their fraction, they should write down where they found it on their index card. Players can also draw a picture of it on their index card. When time is up, players should compare their cards. Whoever found the most examples of his or her fraction wins! Play another round by picking new cards.

Has your child breezed through the activities? If so, he or she can work on this Using Your Head activity independently.

Using Your Head

[25 minutes]

*Grab your **crayons** and **markers**!*

Color the toys in the toy store.

Color $\frac{1}{5}$ of the kites blue.   Color $\frac{1}{3}$ of the tricycles red.

Color $\frac{1}{2}$ of the trucks yellow.   Color $\frac{1}{4}$ of the puzzle pieces green.

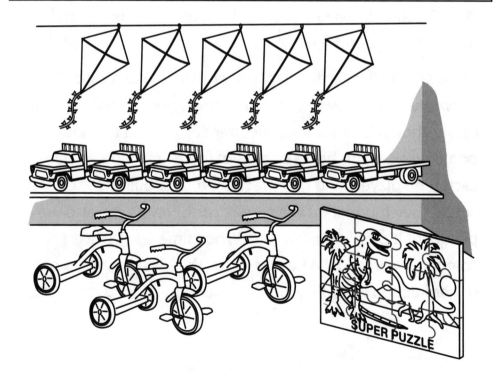

Decimals

Right now, your child doesn't really use decimals in everyday life. There's very little chance your child is going to start using decimals to figure out how to feed the pet or to divvy up TV time with siblings. As a result, your kid might find it boring to learn the basic mechanics of decimals, such as place value and how to read and write decimals.

Encourage your child's interest in decimals by showing how you use decimals with money. Talk about using decimals when you balance your checkbook, or show your child the decimals in the price tags of his favorite toys and clothes. Point out decimals in the world (the weight of food, prices, etc.). Keeping your child's interest will help her learn the vital skills she'll be expected to know.

First things first: Get a sense of what your kid already knows. Turn the page and tell your kid to Jump Right In!

Here's what you'll need for this lesson:
- *grid paper or graph paper*
- *crayons or markers*
- *20 index cards*
- *pencils*

Jump Right In!

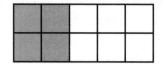

1. What decimal shows the shaded parts of the picture?

    A. 0.04

    B. 0.4

    C. 4.0

    D. 10.4

2. How is "three-hundredths" written as a decimal?

    A. 0.03

    B. 0.3

    C. 3.0

    D. 300

3. What decimal shows how many lollipops are red?

    A. 0.06

    B. 0.4

    C. 0.6

    D. 4.6

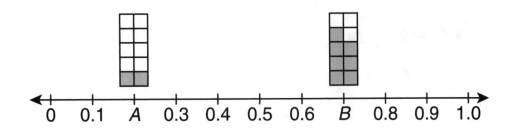

4. What decimal belongs at point *A*? _____

Color in the pictures of socks below to show this decimal.

5. What decimal belongs at point *B*? _____

Color in the pictures of dogs below to show this decimal.

Excellent Job!

 **Checking In**

Ⓐ Answers for pages 172 and 173:

    1. B

    2. A

    3. C

    4. An A+ answer: 0.2; 2 of the 10 socks should be colored in.

    5. An A+ answer: 0.7; 7 of the 10 dogs should be colored in.

Did your child get the correct answers? If so, ask your child to identify the digits in the decimals by place value. For question 2, you could say, "Look at 0.03. What is the place value of the first zero (ones place), the second zero (tenths place), and the three (hundredths place)?"

Did your child get any of the answers wrong? If so, tell your child that the parts of the shapes and groups in these pictures are equal parts. For question 3, say, "Each of these lollipops is an equal part." Tell your child that decimals and fractions deal with equal parts. For each question, ask your child to count the total number of equal parts and then the number of shaded parts.

 **Watch Out!**

Your child is just starting to learn about decimals, so he or she is probably going to struggle with place value. Sometimes, your child might put the digits in any place without attention to place value. For example, your child may not be able to tell the difference between 0.03 and 0.3. Work with your child to show the difference between those numbers. For example, your child can count out 100 beans and write his or her first initial on 3 of them to show 0.03, and then do the same using 10 beans to show 0.3. You can also do this with socks, game pieces, and such.

What to Know...

Review these skills with your child this way:

- A **decimal** is a number that has a decimal point. Decimals include values to the right of the decimal point that are part of a whole number.

- A **digit** is a symbol that is used to write numbers. There are 10 digits: 0, 1, 2, 3, 4, 5, 6, 7, 8, and 9.

- **Place value** is the value of a digit based on its place in a number. For example, in the number 382, the digit 8 is in the tens place, so it has a value of 80.

When your child counts 10 equal parts in a group or a whole, he or she can use decimals to the tenths place.

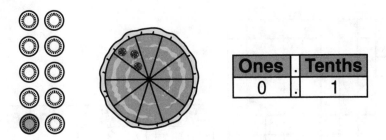

Ones	.	Tenths
0	.	1

Point out to your child that 1 out of 10 game pieces is red. Now, ask your child to count the number of pizza slices with pepperoni and the total number of pizza slices. Then, review the place-value chart with your child.

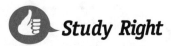 **Study Right**

Make a place-value chart together. Ask your child to write a decimal into the place-value chart, say the decimal out loud, and write the name of the decimal. This kind of practice will help your kid internalize these concepts.

Your child can identify decimals to the tenths place on number lines (and metric rulers).

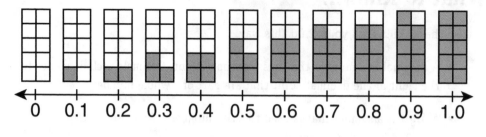

Ask your child to identify the decimal for the shaded parts of each rectangle.

When your child counts 100 equal parts in a group or a whole, he or she can use decimals to the hundredths place.

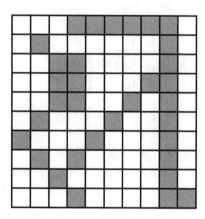

Ones	.	Tenths	Hundredths
0	.	3	3

Ask your child to count the number of equal parts on the game board (100) and the number of shaded parts (33). Then, review the place-value chart with your child.

On Your Way to an "A" Activities

20 { minutes }

Type: Arts and Crafts
Materials needed: grid paper or graph paper, crayons or markers
Number of players: 1

Draw a square on your grid with sides that are 10 squares long. Make sure the square has a total of 100 squares in it. Draw several 10-by-10 squares. Then, make a different design in each one and color in the design so that 0.25 of each square is colored in. See how many different designs you can come up with!

15 { minutes }

Type: Game/Competitive
Materials needed: 20 index cards, pencils
Number of players: 2

Give your partner 10 index cards, and take 10 index cards for yourself. Write a different decimal on each index card. You and your partner should both write 5 decimals to the tenths place and 5 decimals to the hundredths place. Shuffle the cards and place the deck facedown. Take turns picking a card and placing it faceup. The first player to say if the decimal goes to the tenths place or the hundredths place wins a point. Keep playing. The player with the most points at the end wins the game.

Has your child breezed through the activities? If so, he or she can work on this
Using Your Head activity independently.

Using Your Head

Grab your *pencil*!

The shaded pictures below show different decimals. Draw a line from each decimal to its correct picture.

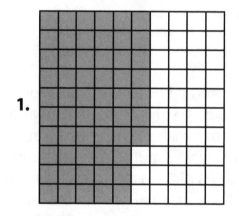

1.   0.7

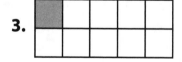

2.   0.1

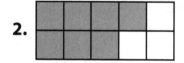

3.   0.57

Adding Decimals

Your kid has probably just learned about how decimals show parts of a whole—those values between 0 and 1. That's a big deal. Now, your kid is on to the next big idea—to regroup (also called "carrying") with decimals. When helping your kid with homework about adding decimals, you might hear him go, "Huh?" And you might be stumped to explain it too.

But as adults, we regroup all the time. Sometimes we call it "making change," when we give 10 pennies for a dime. To regroup, your kid needs to know that 1 one = 10 tenths and 1 tenth = 10 hundredths. Knowing this will help your kid to add decimals correctly as well as with many other tasks, such as making change.

First things first: Get a sense of what your kid already knows. Turn the page and tell your kid to Jump Right In!

Here's what you'll need for this lesson:
- *digital stopwatch*
- *pillowcases or ribbon*
- *chalk*
- *paper*
- *pencils*
- *newspapers*

Jump Right In!

1.   0.14
   + 0.22
   —————

   A. 0.26

   B. 0.34

   C. 0.36

   D. 0.37

2.   0.9
   + 0.4
   —————

   A. 0.13

   B. 1.3

   C. 1.03

   D. 13

3.   0.3
   + 0.5
   —————

   A. 0.08

   B. 0.2

   C. 0.8

   D. 8.0

4.   0.74
   + 0.38
   —————

   A. 0.36

   B. 0.44

   C. 1.02

   D. 1.12

5. Katy bought a stuffed animal that cost $11.45 and a game that cost $5.95. How much did she spend in total?

Excellent Job!

 **Checking In**

ⒶAnswers for page 180:

1. C

2. B

3. C

4. D

5. An A+ answer: "Katy spent $17.40 in total."

Did your child get the correct answers? If so, ask your child to explain how he regrouped with questions 2 and 4.

Did your child get any of the answers wrong? If so, find out where your child was confused. If your child answered questions 1 and 4 incorrectly, then she may be able to add decimals to the tenths but may be confused about adding decimals to the hundredths. If your child answered questions 2 and 3 incorrectly, then she may be able to add decimals without regrouping but may be confused about regrouping. Help your child identify the problem.

Third Graders Are...

Third graders are just beginning to learn about decimals. As a result, when adding decimals together, they may forget to regroup and place digits in the wrong place value. For example, a child might think that 3.8 + 4.7 is 7.15. In this example, the child added the 3 and 4 and wrote the sum to the left of the decimal point, then added 8 and 7 and wrote the sum to the right of the decimal point. Your child might not think about the relationship. Or, he or she might place the decimal in the wrong place: 3.8 + 4.7 = 0.85 or even 85.

What to Know...

Review these skills with your child this way:

- A **decimal** is a number that has a decimal point. Decimals include values to the right of the decimal point that are part of a whole number.

- A **decimal point** is the period in decimals that separates the tenths place and the ones place.

- A **digit** is a symbol that is used to write numbers. There are 10 digits: 0, 1, 2, 3, 4, 5, 6, 7, 8, and 9.

Your child could count money in a piggy bank.

$$\begin{array}{r} \$0.25 \\ + \$0.01 \\ \hline \$0.26 \end{array}$$

$0.25 $0.01

Tell your child to add the digits in the hundredths place first. 5 hundredths + 1 hundredth = 6 hundredths. Then, tell your child to add the digits in the tenths place.

Your child might see a store owner figure out how much someone needs to pay when buying clothes.

$$\begin{array}{r} \$ \overset{1}{9}.\overset{1}{9}9 \\ + \ \$ \ 3.72 \\ \hline \$ \ 13.71 \end{array}$$

Make sure your child can regroup and knows that 9 hundredths + 2 hundredths = 11 hundredths (regroup 11 hundredths to 1 tenth and 1 hundredth). Make sure your child continues to regroup to get the right answer.

On Your Way to an "A" Activities

Type: Game/Competitive
Materials needed: digital stopwatch, pillow-cases or ribbon, chalk, paper, pencils
Number of players: 3 or more

Play "Every Second Counts!" You and the other players will race! Draw a chalk starting line and finish line on the sidewalk. One player is the timer. The other players are the racers. If you have pillowcases, then have a sack race. If you don't, then use the ribbon to have a three-legged race. The timer uses the stopwatch to time each racer and writes down every player's time. Each racer has to complete the race twice. Then, every player adds together his or her two times to find his or her total time. Whoever has the shortest time wins!

Type: Reading/Writing
Materials needed: newspapers, paper, pencils
Number of players: 2 or more

Pretend you are planning a party for someone. Write four lists of what you'll need for the party. Write a "Food" list, a "Decorations" list, a "Games" list, and a "Gifts" list. Each player should take a list. Then, everyone should pretend to shop for things to buy for the party by looking through advertisements in newspapers. (You can also look at the food in your kitchen to find the prices of food.) Each player should write down the prices of everything he or she wants to buy. Then, each player adds his or her costs together. Now, work together to add everyone's costs to find the total cost of the party.

Has your child breezed through the activities? If so, he or she can work on this Using Your Head activity independently.

Using Your Head

{ **10** minutes }

*Grab your **pencil**!*

You are planning a party. Find the costs.

1. _____ + _____ = _____

2. _____ + _____ = _____

3. _____ + _____ = _____
Pizza   Balloon

4. _____ + _____ = _____
Cake   Gift

$0.55 $4.20 $7.45 $2.99 $6.85

Answers: 1. $4.75; 2. $10.44; 3. $7.40; 4. $11.65

Subtracting Decimals

In third grade, your kid is delving into decimals. Not only is your kid asked to identify decimals to the tenths place and hundredths place, but your kid is asked to add and subtract decimals. Your kid may feel that he is spending all his time on decimals. Even if your kid is excited by the challenges of decimals, he may not understand why decimals are so important and so heavily emphasized.

When possible, open your kid's eyes to the large-scale importance of decimals. Decimals are used by musicians, scientists, athletes, and others. Give your kid a sense of the immediate use of decimals. Right now, decimals can help your kid become a better shopper. Learning to subtract decimals means your kid can know how much change she should get when buying snacks or toys. Making purchases is a great way to experience the importance of subtracting decimals.

First things first: Get a sense of what your kid already knows. Turn the page and tell your kid to Jump Right In!

Here's what you'll need for this lesson:
- things around the house
- paper
- pencils
- dimes and pennies
- timer

1. $0.72
    − $0.34

A. 0.38

B. 0.42

C. 0.48

D. 1.06

3.   0.48
    − 0.12

A. 0.36

B. 0.38

C. 0.50

D. 0.60

2.   1.9
    − 0.6

A. 0.3

B. 1.3

C. 1.5

D. 2.5

4.   1.4
    − 0.5

A. 0.1

B. 0.6

C. 0.9

D. 1.9

5. Martin had $0.35 and spent $0.10 on a sticker. How much does he have left?

Excellent Job!

 **Checking In**

Ⓐ Answers for page 186:

1. A

2. B

3. A

4. C

5. An A+ answer: "Martin will have $0.25 left."

Did your child get the correct answers? If so, ask your child to explain how she regrouped with questions 1 and 4.

Did your child get any of the answers wrong? If so, find out where your child was confused. If your child got questions 1 and 3 wrong, then he can subtract decimals to the tenths but may be confused about how to subtract decimals to the hundredths. If your child got questions 1 and 4 wrong, then he can subtract decimals without regrouping, but may be confused when he must regroup.

Third Graders Are...

Third graders sometimes think that they always subtract the "smaller" digit from the "larger" digit, no matter which is above the other in a problem. Check to see if your child made this mistake with questions 1 and 4. Remind your child that in these cases, he or she needs to regroup.

 **Watch Out!**

Third graders are still learning about regrouping when subtracting. As a result, they can easily forget that when they regroup, they are working with digits in different place values. For example, with question 1, your child might remember that she can regroup so that 2 hundredths becomes 12 hundredths. But she may forget that she "took" or "borrowed" 1 tenth in order to do this, and that therefore 7 tenths becomes 6 tenths. Make sure your child remembers that when she regroups she is "taking" or "borrowing" from one place value into another place value. Have her cross out the 7 in the tenths place and write a 6 instead.

What to Know...

Your kid might enjoy the freedom of making his or her own purchases. Knowing how to subtract decimals can help your kid make sure to get correct change.

Review these skills with your child this way:

- A **decimal** is a number that has a decimal point. Decimals include values to the right of the decimal point that are part of the whole number.
- A **decimal point** is the period in decimals that separates the tenths place and the ones place.
- A **digit** is a symbol that is used to write numbers. There are 10 digits: 0, 1, 2, 3, 4, 5, 6, 7, 8, and 9.

Your kid might buy a lollipop with a quarter and get change back.

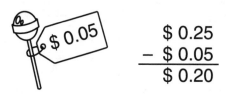

$$\begin{array}{r} \$\ 0.25 \\ -\ \$\ 0.05 \\ \hline \$\ 0.20 \end{array}$$

Ask your child to rewrite the subtraction problem on another piece of paper and make sure he or she lines up the numbers by place value.

$$\begin{array}{r} 1\ 9\ 9\ 10 \\ \$\ 20.00 \\ -\ \$\ 17.95 \\ \hline \$\ 2.05 \end{array}$$

Make sure your child knows how to regroup when there are zeros. Tell him or her to regroup the 2 in the tens place as 1 ten and 10 ones and write a 1 in the tens place. Then, continue: 10 ones = 9 ones + 10 tenths, so your kid can write a 9 in the ones place. Next, 10 tenths = 9 tenths and 10 hundredths, so your kid can write a 9 in the tenths place and a 10 in the hundredths place.

On Your Way to an "A" Activities

Type: Active
Materials needed: things around the house, paper, pencils, dimes, pennies
Number of players: 2 or more

Play "Trader Station." Imagine it's the 1800s. Pretend that you and the other players are getting ready to move west to settle new territories. You need to buy supplies at a Trader Station. Pick out things from the house for the Trader Station. One player should be the trader. The trader should make price tags for each thing using paper and a pencil. The prices should be in whole dollars ($1.00, $2.00, and so on). The other players have to figure out how many dimes to use to buy what they need. Now, play again. This time the prices should be in 10-cent amounts ($0.10, $0.20, and so on). The other players have to figure out how many pennies to use to buy what they need.

Type: Active
Materials needed: paper, pencils, a timer, things around the house
Number of players: 1

Play "Shopping Spree." Pretend that you have won $20.00. Now, find as many things around your house that you can pretend to buy in 5 minutes or less. At the end of 5 minutes, write everything down. Give each thing a price that is a decimal. Subtract one thing from your $20.00. Then, subtract the next thing and the next to see if you have spent all of your $20.00. See how much stuff you can buy before you run out of money!

Has your child breezed through the activities? If so, he or she can work on this Using Your Head activity independently.

Using Your Head

{ **10** minutes }

*Grab a **pencil**!*

Pretend that you and your friends went shopping for school supplies, and you want to see how much money you have left. Use the pictures below to find out.

$ 20.00
—

$ 9.50
—

$ 5.15
—

$14.99

$1.20

$0.45

Answers: $20.00 − $14.99 = $5.01; $9.50 − $1.20 = $8.30; $5.15 − $0.45 = $4.70

Figures and Polygons

There are shapes everywhere your child looks. Your child probably played with shape games as a baby. Back then, your child could feel the shape and look at the shape. Your child didn't have to name the shape. It was simpler stuff—match the blue square with the picture of the blue square. Then, maybe your kid moved on to puzzles involving more intricate shapes, or arts and crafts projects for which your kid could cut out, color, and glue all sorts of shapes.

Shapes are a much more challenging subject for your child now. At this age, your child has to know a whole lot more. Your child is given more and more shapes to sort and classify. The descriptions of the shapes are increasingly more specific. Your child needs to recognize them, name them, and describe them according to the number of sides or angles.

While all this might seem a bit excessive, it's not. We all need to have shared terms for shapes—when someone says "hexagon" or "rectangle," your child has to know what this means. At its core, math is a language. This is some of the key stuff that makes up that language.

First things first: Get a sense of what your kid already knows. Turn the page and tell your kid to Jump Right In!

Here's what you'll need for this lesson:
- *pencils*
- *colored paper*
- *scissors*
- *glue*

Jump Right In!

1. Which picture is <u>not</u> a polygon?

A.

B.

C.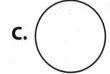

D.

2. Bees build beehives using the shape below. What is this shape?

A. an octagon

B. a hexagon

C. a pentagon

D. a kite

3. Which shape has four equal angles and four equal sides?

A. a square

B. a triangle

C. a pentagon

D. an octagon

Nick and Marta are walking to the playground.

4. Nick sees many things shaped like triangles in the playground. What are two things at the playground shaped like a triangle?

_____

5. Marta sees many different shapes and describes them to Nick. What things in the playground is she describing?

8 angles and 8 sides:

_____

4 square angles and 4 equal sides:

_____

4 angles and 4 sides:

_____

Excellent Job!

 *Checking In*

Answers for pages 192 and 193:

1. C

2. B

3. A

4. An A+ answer: "There are triangles in the swings and jungle gym."

5. An A+ answer: "8 angles and 8 equal sides: stop sign; 4 square angles and 4 sides: bus stop; 4 angles and 4 sides: kites"

Did your child get the correct answers? Did your child remember the names of the shapes? You can ask, "What things can you see right now that are squares? Circles?" And so on.

Did your child get any of the answers wrong? If so, maybe your child is more familiar with some shapes than other shapes. Ask your child to list all the shapes he knows and to draw a picture of each type. Find out what shapes your child knows and doesn't know.

 *Watch Out!*

Sometimes third graders may think that anything with four sides is a square, instead of telling the difference between squares, rectangles, and kites. This is natural. It still means they are noticing that the shape has four sides. Encourage your child to be more specific when describing shapes. Show her examples of squares, rectangles, and kites. Point out that squares have four equal sides, rectangles have two pairs of equal sides and the equal sides are opposite to each other, and kites have two pairs of equal sides and the equal sides share a corner. Ask your child to describe the differences.

What to Know...

Your child sees shapes everywhere.

Review these skills with your child this way:

- An **open figure** is a two-dimensional figure in which there is an opening because not all the sides connect.

- A **closed figure** is a two-dimensional figure in which all the sides connect and there is no opening.

- An **angle** is an open figure formed by two lines that meet at a point.

- A **polygon** is a closed two-dimensional figure with straight sides.

- A **circle** is a round shape with no straight sides. A circle is not a polygon.

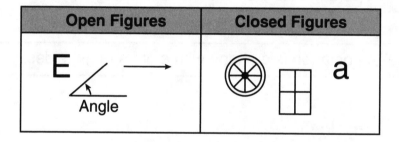

Ask your child to pick out the shapes that are open. Then, pick out the shapes that are closed.

Your kid sees polygons everywhere. Review these skills with your child this way.

○	A circle is a round shape with no straight sides.
△	A triangle is a shape with three straight sides.
□	A square is a shape with four square corners and four straight sides. All the sides are the same length.
▯	A rectangle is a shape with four square corners and four straight sides. The opposite sides of a rectangle are the same length.
◇	A kite is a shape with four angles and four straight sides, and two pairs are equal and touching.
⬠	A pentagon is a shape with five straight sides.
⬡	A hexagon is a shape with six straight sides.
⯃	An octagon is a shape with eight straight sides.

👍 Study Right

Work with your child to create flash cards. Flash cards are a great study tool and can help your child learn about different shapes. On one side of each card, your child can write the name of a shape. On the other side, your child can draw pictures of that shape. This process will help solidify the image of each shape in your child's memory. You and your child can review the cards one by one, or your child can sort them by a specific attribute (polygons vs. non-polygons or open vs. closed). This process will help your child remember and classify many different shapes.

On Your Way to an "A" Activities

20 minutes

Type: Arts and Crafts
Materials needed: colored paper, pencils, scissors, glue
Number of players: 1 or more

Make shape animals. Draw a picture of an animal on a piece of paper. It could be any animal you like (a bunny, a dog, a cat, and so on). Then, cut out shapes, such as squares, rectangles, triangles, and so on, from other pieces of paper. Glue these shapes onto your drawing. Use whatever shape you need to make the animal. For example, you can make the head out of a circle or a square. Make a whole zoo of shape animals!

25 minutes

Type: Game/Competitive
Materials needed: none
Number of players: 3 or more

Play "Secret Shape." Each time you play, one player has to leave the room. While that player is gone, the other players decide on a shape. Then, these players lie on the floor and form the shape with their bodies. Then, call out to the player in the other room to come back in and guess the shape. If the player can't guess the shape, tell the player the shape. Then, this player should give instructions for how to "fix" the shape. Once everyone is agreed that the players on the floor have correctly made the shape, play again. Take turns being the player who leaves the room and has to guess the secret shape.

Using Your Head

Grab your **pencil**!

Use the key to unlock the code. Then, find the answer to the riddle.

C Y I A F N L

1. 4 square angles, 4 equal sides   Letter: _____

2. Round shape, no straight sides   Letter: _____

3. 4 square angles, 4 sides, opposite
sides are equal   Letter: _____

4. 6 angles, 6 straight sides   Letter: _____

5. 5 angles, 5 straight sides   Letter: _____

6. 8 angles, 8 straight sides   Letter: _____

7. 3 angles, 3 straight sides   Letter: _____

What did the kite say to the other shapes?

____ ____ ____ ____ ____ ____ ____ !
 1   2 3 4   5 6 7

Answer: I can fly!

Three-Dimensional Figures

Most kids are familiar with three-dimensional shapes. They have spent their whole lives playing with and manipulating them—blocks, basketballs, building forts, and so on. This provides a strong background and starting point for three-dimensional figures. Even though they have played with and explored these shapes, however, they may not have learned the language that they need to know for math class. They may not know that the corner of a cube is really a "vertex," and they may not care.

In school, it is important to communicate correctly about shapes. So, it becomes more important for your child to be able to name and describe them. Your child may not ever have counted the sides of a cube or looked at the bottom of a cone. But now your child is expected to know what each part of a shape is called and how many there are. The nice thing about this is that shapes are everywhere. Your child can see how understanding shapes is important because people use shapes in their jobs. Engineers, carpenters, artists, and others use shapes. People also use shapes at home and with hobbies: basketball, gardening, cooking, etc.

First things first: Get a sense of what your kid already knows. Turn the page and tell your kid to Jump Right In!

Here's what you'll need for this lesson:
- paper
- pencil
- tape
- glue
- crayons or markers
- things from around the house (juice boxes, canned food, toilet paper rolls, and so on)

Jump Right In!

1. What shape has no straight sides?

   A. a cube

   B. a cylinder

   C. a cone

   D. a sphere

2. What shape is made up of six square faces?

   A. a cube

   B. a cylinder

   C. a cone

   D. a sphere

3. Which of the following pictures best shows a rectangular prism?

   A.

   C.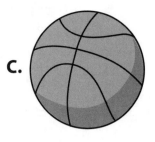

   B.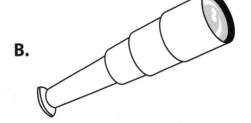

   D.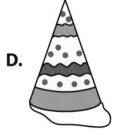

Liz and Derek are building a model of a spacecraft. They are about to glue the rocket booster to the main body.

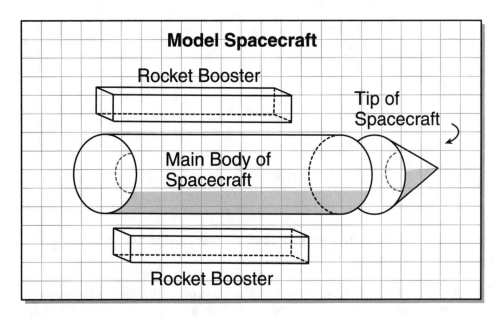

Model Spacecraft

Rocket Booster

Tip of
Spacecraft

Main Body of
Spacecraft

Rocket Booster

4. How many faces does the rocket booster have?

_____

5. How many vertices does the rocket booster have?

_____

6. What shape is the rocket booster?

_____

Excellent Job!

 Checking In

Ⓐ Answers for pages 200 and 201:

    1. D

    2. A

    3. A

    4. An A+ answer: "The rocket booster has 6 faces."

    5. An A+ answer: "The rocket booster has 8 vertices."

    6. An A+ answer: "The rocket booster is a rectangular prism."

Did your child get the correct answers? If so, ask your child to find these shapes in everyday objects around the house.

Did your child get any of the answers wrong? If so, review the incorrect answers. Ask, "How many flat sides does this shape have?" and "How many corners?" Then, explain to your child that the flat sides are called "faces" and the corners are called "vertices."

 Watch Out!

Third graders are just beginning to learn about three-dimensional figures. They are more familiar with two-dimensional shapes, and so they often get them all mixed up. For example, when looking at a sphere, your child might call it a circle. Remind your child that two-dimensional shapes are flat, like a piece of paper. Three-dimensional shapes are solids, like people and furniture. Review the pictures of shapes and ask your child to identify each as a flat or a solid.

What to Know...

Review these skills with your child this way:

- A **two-dimensional figure** has length and width.

- A **three-dimensional figure** has length, width, and height.

- A **face** is a flat side of a three-dimensional figure.

- A **vertex** is a point at which three faces of a three-dimensional figure meet.

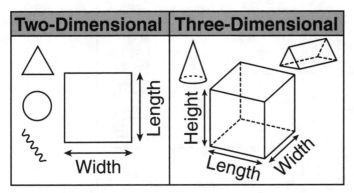

Your child can call two-dimensional shapes "flat shapes" and three-dimensional shapes "solid shapes."

Your child can use solid shapes to build models. Engineers and carpenters need to know the number of faces and vertices in three-dimensional shapes too.

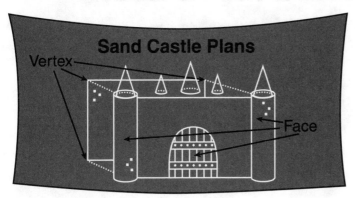

Point out that the corners of the sand castle are called vertices. Then point out that the flat sides are called faces.

Three-Dimensional Figures

Sphere	No straight sides	
Cube	Six square faces, all same size	
Cone	One circular face	
Cylinder	Two circular faces	
Rectangular Prism	Six rectangular faces	
Triangular Prism	Two triangular faces, the same size, and three rectangular faces	

Have your child find these three-dimensional shapes in your home. Ask your child to find as many of each type of three-dimensional shape as possible. Then, look at all of the examples of each type of shape. Have your child count the faces. For example, when looking for rectangular prisms, your child might find a tissue box and a book. Then, your child can count the faces of the tissue box and the book to see that rectangular prisms always have six faces.

Third Graders Are...

Third graders are active and like to learn by exploring with lots of hands-on experience. The nice thing about three-dimensional shapes is that they don't have to be abstract—there are so many examples we can point to around us.

On Your Way to an "A" Activities

20 minutes

Type: Speaking/Listening
Materials needed: paper and pencil
Number of players: 2 or more

Play "Guess My Shape." Pick a three-dimensional shape and describe it, one clue at a time, to the other players. The other players should try to guess the shape with as few clues as possible. When another player correctly guesses the shape, switch roles. The player that guessed correctly picks and describes a three-dimensional shape, and you try to guess it.

30 minutes

Type: Active
Materials needed: things from around the house (juice boxes, canned food, toilet paper rolls, and so on), pencil, tape, glue, crayons or markers
Number of players: 1 or more

Find household materials in different three-dimensional shapes. Write the name of the shape on each thing you find. For example, if you are using a can of food, you would write "cylinder" on it. Then, build something using only household materials. You could build a car from the future, a castle, a spaceship, or something else. Use tape and glue. Color what you built!

Has your child breezed through the activities? If so, he or she can work on this Using Your Head activity independently.

Using Your Head

{ 10 minutes }

*Grab a **pencil**!*

Liz and Derek are going on a Shape Scavenger Hunt. Help them find all the shapes. Write the number of the object you find for each shape.

Sphere _____

Rectangular prism _____

Cube _____

Cylinder _____

Answers: Sphere—2; Rectangular prism—6; Cube—4; Cylinder—1

Cracking the Third Grade

Symmetry

Symmetry is in art, design, music, and nature. Your child sees symmetry in clothing, furniture, advertisements...everywhere! Your child can already tell the difference between an asymmetrical shape, like a blob, and a symmetrical shape, like a star. Now your child is learning how to name what he or she sees as "symmetry."

Not only can symmetry be beautiful, it is also useful. By starting to understand symmetry, your child is starting to understand how to sort, organize, and classify shapes. Your child can also apply symmetry to school projects, sports, and other fields. For example, if your child has ever made a Valentine's Day heart by folding paper and cutting half a heart, then your child has used line symmetry. While it is easy to see how symmetry is useful in arts and crafts, working on symmetry activities is also a great way to introduce your kid to some of the geometry he or she will learn later in school.

First things first: Get a sense of what your kid already knows. Turn the page and tell your kid to Jump Right In!

Here's what you'll need for this lesson:
- pencil
- paper
- paint
- paintbrushes
- scissors
- tape
- mirror
- crayons or markers

Jump Right In!

1. How many lines of symmetry does a square have?

    A. 1

    B. 2

    C. 3

    D. 4

2. Which of these shows the correct line of symmetry?

    A.

    B.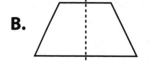

    C.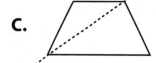

    D.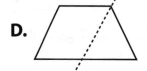

3. Draw the other half of this picture.

Excellent Job!

 **Checking In**

ⒶAnswers for page 208:

1. D

2. B

3. An A+ answer: Your child should have drawn the other half of the "T."

Did your child get the correct answers? If so, ask your child how. Your child may have drawn pictures, mentally imagined the lines of symmetry, solved the problem in parts, or used other problem-solving methods. Tell your child that there are many ways to solve problems. Encourage your child to explore different problem-solving methods.

Did your child get any of the answers wrong? Go back and work on the first question together. Then, ask your child to work on the second question and explain each step he or she takes. If your child does well with the second question, ask your child to finish the third question independently. Then, check your child's work.

 **Watch Out!**

Your child might think that shapes always have only one line of symmetry. But many shapes have more than one line of symmetry (for example, the square in question 1). If your child is confused, cut a square out of paper. Ask your child to fold the square in half to show a line of symmetry. Then, open the square and use a pencil to draw a line where the fold was. Ask your child to fold the square again to find another line of symmetry. Work with your child to see how you can fold the square in four different ways and find four different lines of symmetry (fold top to bottom, side to side, top left corner to bottom right corner, and top right corner to bottom left corner). When you are done, ask your child to count the lines of symmetry you drew with the pencil.

What to Know...

Your child might be just beginning to develop her understanding of the term *symmetry*, but she probably has a practical sense of symmetry from games, arts and crafts, street signs, and everyday life.

Review this skill with your child this way:

- **A line of symmetry** is the fold line for symmetry. If you folded a shape along its line of symmetry, then the two halves would match up. Shapes can have more than one line of symmetry.

Ask your child to point to details in the left half of the house that are the same in the right half of the house. You can fold the drawing along the line of symmetry too.

 **Study Right**

Conducting research can help your child learn. Research symmetry with your child. Use a folder with two pockets. Label the left pocket "Asymmetrical" and the right pocket "Symmetrical." Collect pictures as examples of asymmetrical and symmetrical shapes. Work with your child to identify the shapes and to put them in their proper pocket. Go through the pictures with your child and discuss why one picture has symmetry while another does not.

On Your Way to an "A" Activities

25 minutes

Type: Arts and Crafts
Materials needed: paper, paint, paintbrushes
Number of players: 1

Fold the paper in half, then open it. Paint on one half of the paper. Before the paint is dry, fold the paper again. Rub the paper together. Then, unfold. Some of the paint should have rubbed off so that your painting is now symmetrical!

15 minutes

Type: Art
Materials needed: paper, scissors, tape
Number of players: 2 or more

Play "Starry, starry night." Fold a piece of paper in half. Then, cut out half of a star that includes part of the fold. When you open up the paper, you'll have a whole, symmetrical star. Try again, but this time, fold the paper twice. Cut out part of a star that includes both folds. Try making stars with many folds. Then, hang the stars around your room!

10 minutes

Type: Reading/Writing
Materials needed: paper, pencil, a mirror
Number of players: 1

In the book *Alice in Wonderland*, there is a poem written so that it could be read only in the mirror. Write your first name so that it can be read only in the mirror. Start with one letter at a time and see what it looks like in a mirror. Then, try writing a secret, a story, or a poem that can be read only in a mirror!

Has your child breezed through the activities? If so, he or she can work on this Using Your Head activity independently.

Using Your Head

 [10 minutes]

*Grab a **pencil** and some **crayons** or **markers**!*

Look at the pictures below. Find as many lines of symmetry as you can in each picture. Draw them.

1.

2.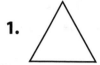

3.

Answers: 1. 3 lines of symmetry; 2. 2 lines of symmetry; 3. 1 line of symmetry

Using Maps

No doubt you have traveled with your child to an unfamiliar destination. Knowing how to find things using a map or a grid is useful in everyday life. Right now, your child uses this skill mainly in math class. But you want your child to develop a good sense of direction and understand how to use maps, if necessary. In the long run, this is a basic, vital skill.

In addition, your child's ability to use maps will help him prepare for higher-level mathematics, specifically for working with coordinate grids. How well your child learns to figure out the relation between things (the library is across the street from the school) can affect how well your child can figure out the relation between lines and parabolas, the sine curve and the y-axis, and so on.

First things first: Get a sense of what your kid already knows. Turn the page and tell your kid to Jump Right In!

Here's what you'll need for this lesson:
- *graph paper*
- *crayons or markers*
- *pencils*
- *number cube*
- *6 index cards*
- *large piece of paper (or small pieces of paper and tape)*

Jump Right In!

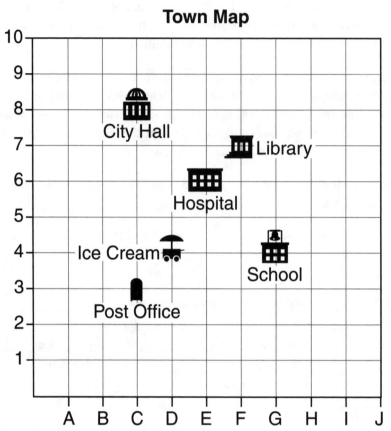

Town Map

1. Where is the library?

    A. F7

    B. C3

    C. F6

    D. E6

2. What is located at E6?

    A. City Hall

    B. the school

    C. the library

    D. the hospital

3. What two buildings are located on line C?

_____

4. What two buildings are located on line 4?

_____

Excellent Job!

 **Checking In**

ⒶAnswers for pages 214 and 215:

> **1.** A

> **2.** D

> **3.** An A+ answer: "The Post Office and City Hall are located on line C."

> **4.** An A+ answer: "The School and the Ice Cream are on line 4."

Did your child get the correct answers? If so, find out what your kid finds easy and what your kid finds difficult about using grids. Ask, "Which of these questions was easiest to answer? Which was hardest to answer?"

Did your child get any of the answers wrong? If so, go over a question together. For example, review question 1. Ask him to put both pointer fingers on the library. Then, move one pointer finger down and one across. Ask your child what letter and number his fingers went to. This is the correct answer.

 **Watch Out!**

Many third graders are inexperienced with maps and grids, so it's easy for them to become confused. Sometimes they think that the name of the place is the location, instead of the picture or point locating the place. For example, your child may have thought that the library was located where the word "Library" appears instead of where the point appears. Tell your child that it's okay to use his or her fingers when working with maps. Your child can put a finger on the picture of the library and then move her finger down the line to find the letter location. Then, your child can put a finger on the picture of the library again and move it to the left to find the number location.

What to Know...

Kids know how to find their way around. They often know secret places in the backyard or neighborhood. Now, your kid is learning how to locate things using maps and grids.

Review this skill with your child this way:

- A **grid** is a pattern of lines that cross each other.

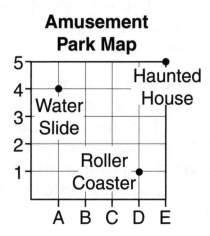

Ask your child to identify the location of each ride at the Amusement Park. Then, ask your child to remember a time when he or she saw or used a map.

 **Study Right**

Sometimes kids learn best by trying something out. Work with your kid to make a map of a room in your house, such as the kitchen. (If you have a room with a tiled floor, then use that room. You and your child can think of the grout between the tiles as the lines of a grid). Then, use the map to give each other directions to places in the room. For example, you might tell your child to move forward 3 lines and to the left 2 lines to find the refrigerator. If you have a map of your neighborhood, use it when you and your child do errands. This will solidify your child's understanding of grids and maps and help him locate places on maps more easily.

On Your Way to an "A" Activities

30 minutes

Type: Game/Competitive
Materials needed: Graph paper, crayons or markers, and pencils
Number of players: 2

Play "Sunken Treasure." You and the other player should each make a map of the ocean. Make the map like the one on page 214 so that you have 10 lines labeled A through J and 10 lines labeled 1 through 10. Put a sunken treasure at a point on your map. Don't show the other player your map.

The goal is to find out where the other player's treasure is before the other player finds out where your treasure is. Do this by taking turns guessing locations of the treasure. For example, say, "I think your treasure is at C3." If you are correct, you win. If not, mark C3 on your map to show that the other player's treasure isn't there. Keep taking turns and guessing locations until someone locates a treasure.

Study Right

When we make connections between what we are learning and what we see around us or already know, we remember more. Help your child make connections to what he or she is learning about maps by pointing out whenever you use or see maps or grids in everyday life. For example, when planning a family trip, bring out the map. Show your child how you locate your destination on the map. Often libraries, museums, zoos, and other vacation sites offer free maps. Make sure to get your child a copy of the map that he or she can use.

Type: Active

Materials needed: a large piece of paper (as large as a rug) or small pieces of paper and tape, a number cube, 6 index cards, pencils

Number of players: 2 or more

Make your own playing area. Create a large grid using a very large piece of paper. Along the bottom of the paper, write the letters A through F. Draw lines from these letters across the paper. On the side of the paper, write the numbers 1 through 6. Draw lines from these numbers across to the other side.

Then, write the letters A through F on the index cards so that there is one letter on each index card. Shuffle the cards and put them facedown. Make the first round the "Left Foot" round. The first player picks the top card and rolls the number cube. This player has to move his or her left foot to this location. For example, if the player picked an F and rolled a 5, this player should put his or her left foot at F5. Next, all the other players play by picking cards and rolling the number cube. Keep playing. Each round can be different (right foot, left hand, right hand). Whoever can stay the longest without falling wins!

Has your child breezed through the activities? If so, he or she can work on this Using Your Head activity independently.

Using Your Head

[**10**]
minutes

*Grab a **pencil** and some **crayons** or **markers**!*

Draw each building on the map where it should be.

Grocery store: C5	Gas station: E10
School: D1	Zoo: G1
Art store: A8	Pizza parlor: J2

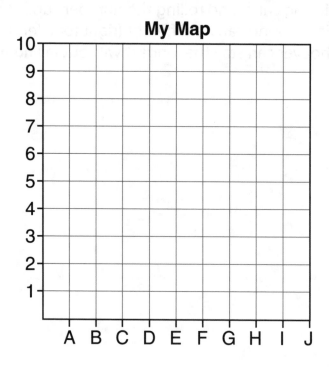

My Map

Slides, Flips, and Turns

Slides, flips, and turns occur constantly around us in everyday life. Your child also studies them in math class. And yet, your child might not realize that the stuff of everyday life and math class are connected. Sometimes kids don't know how to connect their everyday experiences with what they learn in math class. Your child might not realize that the examples of slides, flips, and turns in math class are examples—not the only ways these things can occur. As a result, if your child is shown a picture of a triangle turning, he might just resign himself to thinking that all examples of turns involve triangles or happen in math class. Your kid might not know that the computer graphics in video games and animated films are created using slides, flips, and turns. Your kid might not realize that the turning of a tire on a bike is, in fact, an example of a turn.

Help your child learn that the terms *slide*, *flip*, and *turn* don't describe the shapes used in the examples—they describe the way the shapes were moved. Your child knows how to slide (at the slide in the park), flip (as in flipping a coin or watching an acrobat flip), and turn (turn the wheel of a bike). Now, your child needs to connect this knowledge to the geometric shapes and coordinate grids in math class.

First things first: Get a sense of what your kid already knows. Turn the page and tell your kid to Jump Right In!

Here's what you'll need for this lesson:
- *pencils*
- *crayons or markers*

Jump Right In!

1. Which picture shows a flip?

 A.

C.

B.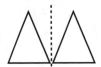

D.

2. Which picture shows a slide?

A.

C.

 B.

D.

3. Which picture shows a turn?

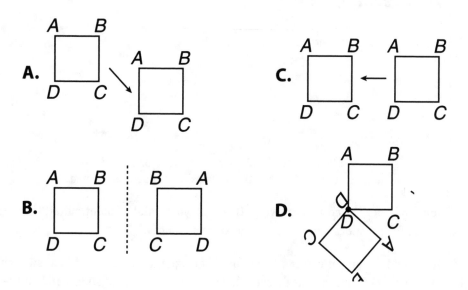

4. Draw your favorite animal. Now, draw how the picture of your animal looks after you slide, flip, or turn it.

Excellent Job!

 **Checking In**

❹Answers for pages 222 and 223:

1. B

2. C

3. D

4. An A+ answer: Your child should draw a picture of an animal and then draw how the picture would look after it was slid, flipped, or turned.

Did your child get the correct answers? If so, ask your child to point out all the examples of flips, slides, and turns in the answer choices.

Did your child get any of the answers wrong? If so, point out that all the answer choice Bs are examples of flips, all the answer choice Cs are examples of slides, and all the answer choice Ds are examples of turns. Ask your child to look at each set of pictures and describe the difference between a slide, a flip, and a turn.

 **Watch Out!**

Sometimes, children at this age don't pay enough attention to all the details. A child may not look at the labels assigned to the corners of a square, for instance. He or she may not notice if those labels are in the same place (for a slide) or mirror images of what they were before (for a flip). Explain to your child why it is important to look at all the labels. Children may not be able to differentiate otherwise.

Cut out a square and label the corners A, B, C, and D. Practice turning the square to show that the letters stay in the same order with respect to each other but move as the square moves. Next, flip the square and show how the letters are a mirror image of where they were before the flip. Finally, slide the square to show that the letters stay in the same order with respect to each other, but move as the square moves.

What to Know...

Review these skills with your child this way:

- To **slide** a shape means to move it along a line.

- To **flip** a shape means to move it over a line.

- To **turn** a shape means to move it around a point.

- This is a **line.** ←——————→

- This is a **point.** ●

Your child has to slide, flip, and turn shapes when playing with a puzzle of outer space.

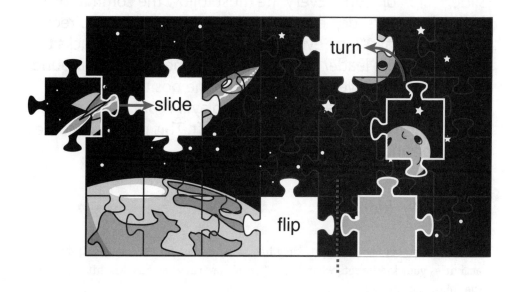

Ask your child to use a puzzle piece to practice sliding, flipping, and turning.

On Your Way to an "A" Activities

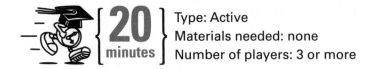

[20 minutes]

Type: Active
Materials needed: none
Number of players: 3 or more

Play "Twist and Shout, Now Slide, Flip, Turn, and Shout." Everyone stands in a group. One player gets to be the leader and stands in front, facing everyone. The leader makes a funny shape with her body and face. This means the leader could wrinkle her nose, scratch her armpits, balance on one leg, or anything else. Then, the leader gives the group a command by saying "slide," "flip," or "turn." Everyone must follow the command. If the leader says "slide," everyone must move in a single direction. If the leader says "flip," everyone must turn with their backs to the leader. If the leader says "turn," everyone must spin around. While doing this, everyone must keep the position the leader had. If anyone makes a mistake, that player is out of the game. Keep playing until only one person is left. This person becomes the leader, and the game starts again.

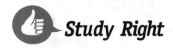

Study Right

Often, kids remember best the stuff they had to figure out for themselves. If during the activities your kid forgets what "slide," "flip," or "turn" means, ask him or her to try the following things:

- Talk about the terms with the other players. Do any of the other players know what these terms mean?

- Look it up in this book.

- Practice using shapes to figure out what the terms mean.

If your child is still confused, then help him or her look up the terms in this book to find the answers.

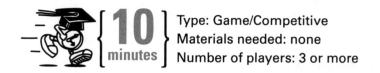

Type: Game/Competitive
Materials needed: none
Number of players: 3 or more

Play "Clues." Begin by playing a "Turn" round. Each player has to think of an example of a turn. Then, this player gives clues to the other players. The other players have to figure it out. For example, a player might realize that the movement of a tire on a car is an example of a turn. This player might give the clues "I'm round," "I'm on a car," and "I'm made of rubber." The first player to figure out the example gets a point.

Once every player has used their example of a turn, move on to the "Slide" round and the "Flip" round. At the end, the player with the most points wins.

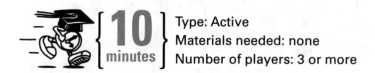

Type: Active
Materials needed: none
Number of players: 3 or more

Play "How Good Is Your Memory?" One player gets to be "It." This player looks at everything in the room and then leaves the room. Then, other players move three things in the room. They must move things to show a turn, a flip, and a slide. For example, they could turn a pillow, flip a book, and slide a lamp over a few inches. Then, "It" comes back and has to find the three things that were changed. If this player has difficulty, the other players can give hints. Once all three things are identified, everything in the room should be put back into place. Then, a different player gets to be "It."

Has your child breezed through the activities? If so, he or she can work on this Using Your Head activity independently.

Using Your Head

[**10** minutes]

*Grab a **pencil** and some **crayons** or **markers**!*

- These puzzle pieces have to be slid, flipped, or turned to fit correctly into the puzzle. Figure out what has to be done.

1. _____

2. _____

3. _____

Answers: 1. Slide; 2. Flip; 3. Turn

Patterns with Shapes

Kids make sense of patterns very early on. Patterns in sounds allow them to learn language. Routines help them learn how to navigate their way around in the world. And kids naturally notice patterns. Your kid knows that the seasons follow a pattern: spring, summer, fall, winter. Also, if your kid sees shoelaces with a printed pattern that goes, "pencil, book, pencil, book," then your kid probably knows that the rule is "pencil, book."

But now your child is working with more complicated patterns. As your kid grows, he'll become ready to handle these extra details. But first he has to learn that these details are important. And he has to learn how to tap into all his natural energy to focus on the details in complicated patterns. For example, your child might notice extra details in a pattern on shoelaces, like "little pencil, little book, big pencil, big book." He might not have paid attention to these details before. And as you know, little details are important. Honing your child's ability to process these details can make a big difference!

First things first: Get a sense of what your kid already knows. Turn the page and tell your kid to Jump Right In!

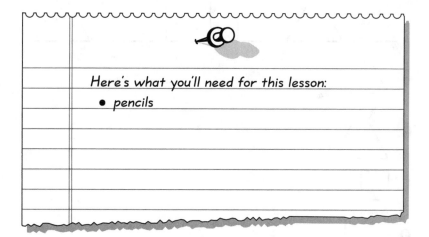

Here's what you'll need for this lesson:
- pencils

Jump Right In!

1. What is the next shape in this pattern?

    A. a square

    B. a triangle

    C. a hexagon

    D. an octagon

2. What shape is missing from this pattern?

    A. △

    B. △

    C. ▫

    D. ☐

Ryan and Kiki are making bookmarks with stickers.

3. Look at Ryan's bookmark. What is the rule for the pattern on Ryan's bookmark?

_____

Draw the shape that will happen next.

4. Look at Kiki's bookmark. What is the rule for the pattern on Kiki's bookmark?

_____

Draw the shape that is missing.

Excellent Job!

 *Checking In*

Ⓐ Answers for pages 230 and 231:

1. B

2. A

3. An A+ answer: "The rule for Ryan's bookmark is 1 swirl shape, 1 big smiley face, 1 little smiley face. There will be a swirl shape next."

4. An A+ answer: "The rule for Kiki's bookmark is 2 bananas, 1 monkey. The shape that is missing is a banana."

Did your child get the correct answers? If so, ask your child to name the rule for each of the patterns. Make sure your child can name the rule and didn't just guess the correct answers. You can also ask your child to draw the next several shapes in each pattern.

Did your child get any of the answers wrong? If so, ask him to identify the rule for each pattern. If your child does this incorrectly, then he has difficulty with identifying the rules to patterns. If your child identifies the rules correctly, then he may have difficulty applying the rule to predict the next shape or to identify a missing shape in a pattern.

 *Watch Out!*

Sometimes kids rush to identify the rule to a pattern before really looking at all the shapes in the pattern. For example, with question 4, your child may have looked only at the first few shapes in the pattern and identified the wrong answer as a result. Explain to your child that shapes repeat in a pattern. Using question 4, say, "There are 2 bananas followed by a monkey. Then, there is another banana, which starts the pattern over again." Instruct your child to circle the 2 bananas followed by the monkey, and explain to your child that "2 bananas, 1 monkey" is the rule.

What to Know...

Your child sees patterns all around—in paper towels, furniture, rugs, wallpaper, clothes, and so on.

Review these skills with your child this way:

- A **pattern** is a series of numbers, figures, or pictures that follows a rule.

- A **rule** is a statement that tells how the items in a pattern are related.

You or your child might have clothes with patterns like these.

Rule: Bird, Tree, Nest

Ask your child to circle the repeating shapes. Tell your child that this is the pattern.

 *Checking In*

Make sure your child understands how to use a rule to predict the next shape in a pattern. Explain that the last shape on the scarf is a nest, so the next shape would be the first shape in the pattern. Ask your child to predict the next shape that should happen (bird).

You and your child might see a sign with a pattern that is missing a piece.

Point out to your child that there is a shape missing in the pattern (right before the last balloon). Ask your child to look at the pattern and circle the repeating shapes. Tell your child that the shapes that repeat make up the rule to the pattern. Now, ask your child to identify the missing shape (party hat).

 **Checking In**

Make sure your child understands how to use a rule to identify a missing shape. Point out that the missing shape falls between a cake and a balloon. Ask your child, "What comes after the cake and before the balloon in the rule for this pattern?" (Party hat)

Third Graders Are...

Third graders are natural observers, but their observations still need to be refined. Your kid may observe a shape without paying attention to the size of the shape or its color. Perhaps she observes the size but not the shape or color. Your kid needs practice and experience comparing and contrasting things so these subtleties are observed.

On Your Way to an "A" Activities

Type: Game/Competitive
Materials needed: none
Number of players: 2

Play the game "I Spy" with shapes. You can play this game anywhere (at home, at school, in the car). Look for any kind of pattern. When you see one, you can say, "I spy a pattern with circles." The other player then needs to see where the pattern is and find a new one with different shapes.

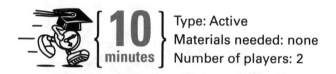

Type: Active
Materials needed: none
Number of players: 2

One player describes a pattern of behavior: jump twice, hop once, jump twice, hop once. The other player performs this pattern. Then, switch roles.

Has your child breezed through the activities? If so, he or she can work on this Using Your Head activity independently.

Using Your Head

[15 minutes]

Grab a pencil!

Ryan and Kiki are now making collars for their cats and dog. Draw the shapes needed to finish the patterns.

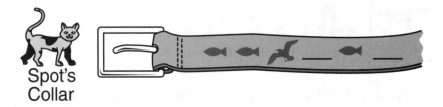

Spot's Collar

Waggy's Collar

Mitten's Collar

Answers: Spot's collar—a fish, a bird; Waggy's collar—a black diamond, a white circle; Mitten's collar—a white mitten, a smiley face

Patterns with Numbers

You and your child began exploring number patterns years ago. When you first taught your child to count 1, 2, 3, ..., you were teaching her a number pattern. The rule for this pattern is simple—she just has to add one to the previous number. Perhaps you haven't talked about this pattern in depth, but undoubtedly you have helped your child learn her numbers, and you didn't skip any.

But there are many more patterns in the world. Some are natural. For example, there is a type of cicada that comes out to mate only every 17 years! There are some man-made patterns in the world too. For example, box seating at a stadium may be numbered by 5s (Box 5, Box 10, Box 15, and so on). Houses may be numbered in a pattern with the rule "add 2" (124 Oak Lane, 126 Oak Lane, 128 Oak Lane, and so on). Sometimes, your kid has to figure out the number that is missing or the number that will come next. To do this, your kid needs to know how to figure out the relationship between numbers in a pattern.

First things first: Get a sense of what your kid already knows. Turn the page and tell your kid to Jump Right In!

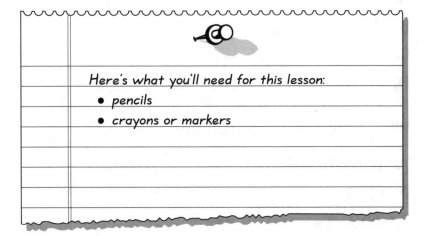

Here's what you'll need for this lesson:
- *pencils*
- *crayons or markers*

Jump Right In!

1. What number is missing from this pattern?

12, 14, 16, _____, 20, 22

A. 14

B. 16

C. 18

D. 24

2. What is the next number in this pattern?

11, 14, 17, 20, _____

A. 8

B. 18

C. 19

D. 23

3. What is the rule for this pattern?

22, 18, 14, 10, 6, 2

A. add 4

B. subtract 4

C. add 2

D. subtract 3

Drake and Candice were going to order a set of comic books. They needed to figure out how long it would take for their comic books to be delivered, but their order form was damaged.

Number of Comic Books	1	2	3	4	5	6	7	8
Days to Ship	3	5	7		11	13	15	

4. Look at the number of shipping days. These numbers form a pattern. What is the rule to this pattern?

_____

5. If Drake and Candice ordered 4 comic books, how many days would it take for the comic books to ship?

_____

6. If Drake and Candice ordered 8 comic books, how many days would it take for the comic books to ship?

_____

 **Excellent Job!**

Checking In

Ⓐ Answers for pages 238 and 239:

1. C

2. D

3. B

4. An A+ answer: Add 2

5. An A+ answer: 9

6. An A+ answer: 17

Did your child get the correct answers? If so, ask, "Did you figure out the answer and then look at the answer choices? Or did you look at the answer choices and pick the one that fit best?" If the latter, ask your child to look at each question again, cover up the answer choices with his hand, and find the answers.

Did your child get any of the answers wrong? If so, review finding and applying the rules to patterns. Ask your child to identify the rule for question 1. Explain that the rule describes the relationships between the numbers. So, for example, with question 1, adding 2 to the first number gets the second number (12 + 2 = 14). This is true of all the numbers in a pattern (14 + 2 = 16, 20 + 2 = 22). Now, explain that to find the missing number, you have to add 2 to the number before it. Ask your child to find the answer to 16 + 2.

Watch Out!

Some third graders have seen patterns only with addition rules, and they may not realize that patterns can also be made using subtraction. Review question 3 with your child. Point out that the numbers get smaller, so addition can't be the rule. Ask your child what she would do to 22 to get 18 (subtract 4). Then, check this rule by making sure it can be used to get the other numbers in the pattern.

What to Know...

Review these skills with your child this way:

- A **pattern** is a series of numbers, figures, or pictures that follows a rule.

- A **rule** is a statement that tells how the items in a pattern are related.

Your kid might have read about a type of cicada that comes out once every three years.

Years cicadas were seen: 1992, 1995, 1998, 2001, _____, 2007

Ask your child what to do to 1995 to get 1998 (add 3 years). Tell her to check to see if she can get the other years this same way, and if so, then this is the rule. Ask your child to use the rule to find the missing year (2004).

Your kid might see birdhouses at the park.

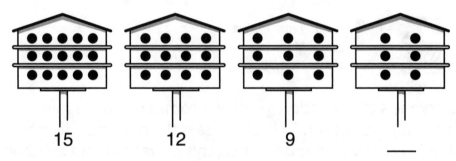

| 15 | 12 | 9 | ___ |

Rule: Subtract 3

Ask your child if the number of holes in the birdhouses is increasing (addition) or decreasing (subtraction). Then, ask your child to use the rule to find out how many holes there are for birds in the last birdhouse (6).

On Your Way to an "A" Activities

{ **10** minutes } Type: Active
Materials needed: none
Number of players: 2 or more

The first player thinks of a pattern. The pattern should involve addition. This player can clap out the pattern. Then, the other players need to identify the rule. For example, the first player may have clapped 3 times, 5 times, and 7 times. Then, the other players would have to identify the rule as "add 2." The first player to identify the rule gets to be the one to clap a new pattern. Keep playing until everyone has had a chance to clap a pattern.

{ **10** minutes } Type: Active
Materials needed: none
Number of players: 3 or more

Everyone sits in a circle. One player comes up with a rule involving subtraction. This player says the rule and a number (it should be a large number). Then, this player calls out another player's name. The player called on has to say the next number in the rule and call out a different player's name. For example, Tim might say, "Subtract 3, 24, Sally." Then, Sally would subtract 3 from 24 and pick another player, "21, Bill." Bill would continue. Keep playing until you can't continue the pattern or until everyone has had a chance.

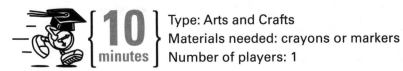

Type: Arts and Crafts
Materials needed: crayons or markers
Number of players: 1

Come up with a rule using addition. Starting with 1 or 2, figure out all the numbers in this pattern up to 100. Color these numbers in. Look at the design you made.

1	2	3	4	5	6	7	8	9	10
11	12	13	14	15	16	17	18	19	20
21	22	23	24	25	26	27	28	29	30
31	32	33	34	35	36	37	38	39	40
41	42	43	44	45	46	47	48	49	50
51	52	53	54	55	56	57	58	59	60
61	62	63	64	65	66	67	68	69	70
71	72	73	74	75	76	77	78	79	80
81	82	83	84	85	86	87	88	89	90
91	92	93	94	95	96	97	98	99	100

Now, come up with a rule using subtraction. Starting with 99 or 100, figure out all the numbers in this pattern. Color these numbers in. Look at the design you made.

1	2	3	4	5	6	7	8	9	10
11	12	13	14	15	16	17	18	19	20
21	22	23	24	25	26	27	28	29	30
31	32	33	34	35	36	37	38	39	40
41	42	43	44	45	46	47	48	49	50
51	52	53	54	55	56	57	58	59	60
61	62	63	64	65	66	67	68	69	70
71	72	73	74	75	76	77	78	79	80
81	82	83	84	85	86	87	88	89	90
91	92	93	94	95	96	97	98	99	100

Has your child breezed through the activities? If so, he or she can work on this Using Your Head activity independently.

Using Your Head

{ **10** minutes }

*Grab a **pencil**!*

Draw a line from each pattern to its rule.

1. 3, 7, 11, 15, . . .   **A.** Subtract 2

2. 19, 16, 13, . . .   **B.** Add 4

3. 26, 31, 36, . . .   **C.** Subtract 3

4. 12, 10, 8, . . .   **D.** Add 5

Answers: 1. B; 2. C; 3. D; 4. A

Length and Perimeter

Measurement is one of those concepts in which children are naturally interested. Children often want to know who is taller and who is shorter. As they get older, they refine their measurement skills and begin using the tools of measurement. Kids are interested in these tools. Using rulers and tape measures to measure in different units gives them a sense of satisfaction.

In math class, your kid might learn about different units. At home, your kid can further explore measuring with different units. Your kid can continue measuring his height, but he also can measure other things around the house—how much wrapping paper is needed to go around a gift, how high up to put the basketball hoop, and so on. Not only are these pretty interesting things to your kid, but measuring stuff at home gives your kid concrete experiences applying his new skills.

First things first: Get a sense of what your kid already knows. Turn the page and tell your kid to Jump Right In!

Here's what you'll need for this lesson:

- *paper*
- *pencils*
- *ruler with both American units and metric units*
- *string*
- *books of varying sizes*
- *chalk*

Jump Right In!

Jay and Celia have plans for building a birdhouse.

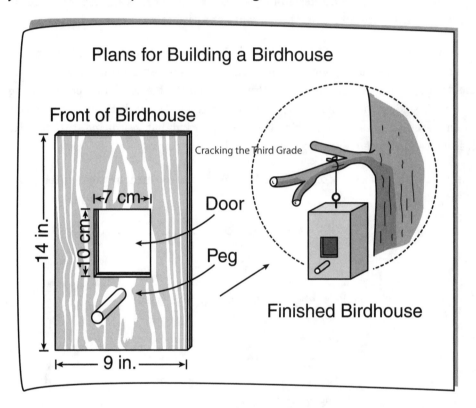

Plans for Building a Birdhouse

Front of Birdhouse

14 in.

|←7 cm→|

|←10 cm→|

9 in.

Door

Peg

Cracking the Third Grade

Finished Birdhouse

1. The birdhouse project came with 1 meter of thick string. How many centimeters are in 1 meter?

   A. 3 centimeters

   B. 12 centimeters

   C. 36 centimeters

   D. 100 centimeters

2. Celia cut 1 yard of rope. How many inches are in 1 yard?

   A. 12 inches

   B. 24 inches

   C. 36 inches

   D. 100 inches

3. Jay glued the peg below the doorway. How long is the peg?

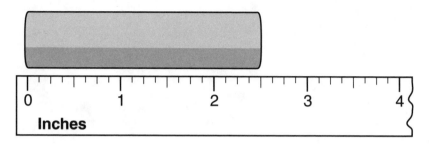

A. 2 inches

B. $2\frac{1}{2}$ inches

C. $3\frac{1}{2}$ inches

D. 4 inches

4. The front of the birdhouse is 14 inches by 9 inches. What is the perimeter of the front of the birdhouse?

_____

5. The door to the birdhouse is 10 centimeters by 7 centimeters. What is the perimeter of the door to the birdhouse?

_____

Excellent Job!

 **Checking In**

ⒶAnswers for pages 246 and 247:

    1. D

    2. C

    3. B

    4. An A+ answer: 46 inches

    5. An A+ answer: 34 centimeters

Did your child get the correct answers? If so, ask your child to share her experiences measuring length. Has she measured in inches, centimeters, meters, and yards—or only with inches?

Did your child get any of the answers wrong? If so, which ones? Your child might need a review of the following: using a ruler, converting between American units, converting between metric units, and/or finding perimeter. Start out by reviewing how to use a ruler. Point out that the left edge of the peg in question 1 lines up with the 0 on the ruler. Then, tell your child to put his finger on the right end of the peg and move his finger down to the ruler to find the peg's length.

Watch Out!

Some third graders have measured things only to the whole inch or whole centimeter. Your child may not be familiar with measuring to the half inch or half centimeter. If your ruler is wooden, guide your child to label all the half-inch or half-centimeter marks correctly ($\frac{1}{2}$ in., $1\frac{1}{2}$ in., $2\frac{1}{2}$ in., etc., and $\frac{1}{2}$ cm, $1\frac{1}{2}$ cm, $2\frac{1}{2}$ cm, respectively). If your ruler is plastic, put a piece of masking tape below the measurement marks and have your child write on the tape.

What to Know...

Review these skills with your child this way:

- The **American system of measurement** is a system of measurement commonly used in the United States. Inch, foot, and yard are units of length in the American system of measurement.

- The **metric system of measurement** is a system of measurement used around the world. Centimeter and meter are units of length in the metric system of measurement.

- **Perimeter** is the measure of the distance around a figure. To find the perimeter, you can add together the length of all the sides of the figure.

Your child could measure to find the perimeter of a camping badge.

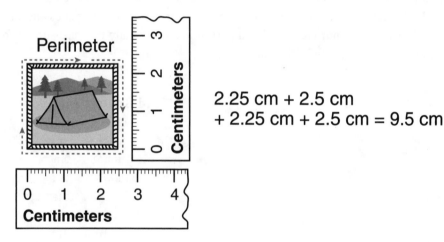

2.25 cm + 2.5 cm
+ 2.25 cm + 2.5 cm = 9.5 cm

Ask your child to find the length of the bottom of the badge and the side of the badge. Then, ask your child to find the perimeter.

 *Checking In*

When shown the length of two sides of a rectangle, your kid might forget to add the lengths of all four sides to find the perimeter. Remind your child that the opposite sides of a rectangle are equal. Then, have your kid use this information to label the length of each side of the badge in the picture.

American Units	Metric Units
12 inches = 1 foot	
36 inches = 1 yard	100 centimeters = 1 meter
3 feet = 1 yard	

Take out an inch ruler. Ask your kid to count out the number of inches in a foot and in a yard. Then, take out a meter ruler and ask your kid to count out the number of centimeters in a meter.

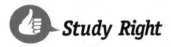 **Study Right**

Practice makes perfect. Provide your child with plenty of practice using American units and metric units. Often, kids love to measure how they grow, so keep a chart of your child's growth. Ask your child to measure his or her height in inches and in centimeters. Then, ask your child to find a part of his or her body that measures 1 foot, 1 meter, or 1 yard. List these in the chart too.

Third Graders Are...

Third graders are developing their motor control and hand-eye coordination. So, using a ruler to measure down to the half inch or quarter inch can sometimes be quite a process! Encourage your kid to keep trying. If your kid has difficulty measuring to a quarter inch, let him mark the ruler with a pencil and then look at the measurement or measure things that are easier (such as putting the ruler on a table to measure a fork, instead of holding up a ruler to measure a lampshade).

On Your Way to an "A" Activities

{20 minutes}

Type: Active
Materials needed: ruler, books of varying sizes, string, a pencil
Number of players: 1

You can find the perimeter of the cover of a book. With one hand, hold an end of the string to the edge of the cover. Then, wrap the string around the edges of the cover until it meets your hand. Pinch the end of the string. Mark this point on the string with a pencil. Then, measure the string to the mark.

{10 minutes}

Type: Arts and Crafts
Materials needed: Chalk, paper, pencil, ruler
Number of players: 2 or more

Go outside when it's sunny. One player should stand in the sun so that there is a shadow. The other player draws a chalk line around the shadow. Then, switch turns so each player's shadow is drawn in chalk. Now, measure the length of the shadows. Write down the lengths on a piece of paper. Do this again a few other times later in the day. Notice how the lengths of your shadows change!

Has your child breezed through the activities? If so, he or she can work on this Using Your Head activity independently.

Using Your Head

[**10** minutes]

*Grab a **pencil**!*

How long do you think each thing is? Take your best guess. Then, draw a line to match each thing with its length.

1. The length of a football field

2. The width of a spider

3. The perimeter of a pool

4. The width of a chair

A. about 10 meters

B. about 2 cm

C. about 100 yards

D. about 2 feet

Answers: 1. C; 2. B; 3. A; 4. D

Charts and Graphs

Everywhere your kid looks—in books, in magazines, in newspapers, on television—there are charts and graphs organizing information. It is both common and useful to organize information in this way. That is why it's important for your kid to be able to read the information in charts and graphs. It's also important for your child to be able to create a chart or graph to convey information.

Charts and graphs are not just for school. They are used in research and development, scientific research, and business. They are so ubiquitous, in fact, that if your child asks, "When will we ever use this outside of school?" you can easily answer by simply opening a newspaper or magazine and finding the charts and graphs used in it.

First things first: Get a sense of what your kid already knows. Turn the page and tell your kid to Jump Right In!

Here's what you'll need for this lesson:
- *pencil*
- *paper*
- *crayons or markers*
- *sports game on TV, board game, or video game*
- *poster paper*
- *tape*
- *string*

Jump Right In!

Player	Number of Baskets
Fran	ⵌ l
Joe	ll
Louis	ⵌ lll
Denise	llll
Collin	llll

1. Who scored the most baskets?

A. Fran

B. Louis

C. Denise

D. Collin

2. How many baskets did Denise score?

A. 4

B. 6

C. 7

D. 8

3. Which two players scored the same number of baskets?

A. Denise and Collin

B. Fran and Joe

C. Louis and Denise

D. Fran and Louis

4. Look at the tally chart on page 254. Complete the pictograph below to show the same information.

Player's Baskets

Player	Number of Baskets
Fran	
Joe	
Louis	
Denise	
Collin	

Key  = 2 baskets

5. Now, complete the bar graph below to show the same information.

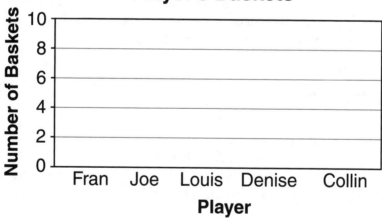

Excellent Job!

 **Checking In**

❹Answers for pages 254 and 255:

1. B

2. A

3. A

4. An A+ answer: Your child should draw 3 basketballs for Fran, 1 basketball for Joe, 4 basketballs for Louis, 2 basketballs for Denise, and 2 basketballs for Collin.

5. An A+ answer: Your child should draw a bar to 6 for Fran, a bar to 2 for Joe, a bar to 8 for Louis, a bar to 4 for Denise, and a bar to 4 for Collin.

Did your child get the correct answers? If so, find out if your child looked at all the information in the charts and graphs or just the information needed to find the correct answer. Ask, "What is the title of the bar graph for question 5? How are each of the bars labeled? What other words do you see?" Make sure your child practices looking at all the information.

Did your child get any of the answers wrong? If your child answered question 1, 2, or 3 wrong, then make sure she realizes that a set of 4 tally marks bundled with a hash mark across them represents 5. If your child answered question 4 wrong, then she might have assumed that 1 basketball represents 1 basket. Point out the key in the pictograph. If your child answered question 5 wrong, then she might not have paid attention to the numbers on the graph. Review the questions together.

 **Watch Out!**

Sometimes, third graders forget to follow all the steps. Tell your child to create a list of steps necessary to answer a question. Then, have him follow his own list. For example, for question 4, your kid may have remembered to use the key sometimes, but not all the time. Your kid could write a list of steps like the following:

- Look at the name on the tally chart.
- Find out the number of baskets.
- Use the key to figure out how many basketballs I should draw.
- Draw the baskets next to the same name in the pictograph.

Now, your kid just needs to look at the steps for every name in the pictograph.

What to Know...

Your kid has probably seen charts and graphs in the newspaper and at school.

Review tally charts with your child this way:

- A **tally** is a way of counting by making a mark for each item counted.

- A **tally chart** is a table that shows data with tally marks.

You and your kid might use a tally chart at home to show information.

Fruits and Vegetables Eaten Today

Person	Servings
Mom |卌	
Dad	|||||
Brother	|||||
Me	卌 |||

Ask your child to count the number of tally marks to find out how many servings "Mom" ate today. Do the same for the other people in the chart.

Review pictographs and bar graphs with your child this way:

- A **pictograph** is a graph that shows data by using picture symbols. Each pictograph has a key that tells how many items each symbol represents.

- A **bar graph** is a graph that shows data by using bars of different sizes.

Your kid also may have seen pictographs and bar graphs.

Fruits and Vegetables Eaten Today

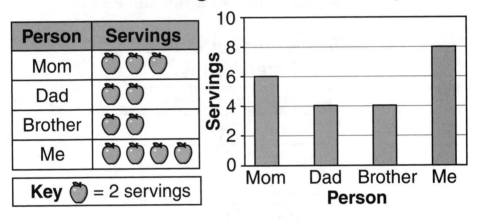

Person	Servings
Mom	🍎 🍎 🍎
Dad	🍎 🍎
Brother	🍎 🍎
Me	🍎 🍎 🍎 🍎

Key 🍎 = 2 servings

· · · · · · · · · · · · · ·
Ask your kid to figure out how many servings "Mom" ate, as shown in the pictograph. Then, check out the bar graph.

 *Checking In*

Did your child forget to look at the pictograph's key? If so, practice using the key with your child. Point out that "Mom" has 3 apples, and each apple means 2 servings. So, count the apples by 2s (2, 4, 6) to show that "Mom" had 6 servings. Now, ask your kid to count by 2s to find out how many servings the brother had (4).

On Your Way to an "A" Activities

Type: Reading/Writing

Materials needed: paper, pencils, crayons or markers, as well as a sports game on TV, a board game, or a video game

Number of players: 2 or more

This is a good activity for when you are watching a sports game or playing a game. If you are watching a sports game, each player should pick his or her favorite athlete. Draw a tally chart like the one on page 257. Then, fill in the tally chart with the names of the athletes. While watching the game, write tally marks to show the number of points each athlete scored. If you are playing a game, write the name of each player in the tally chart. Then, write tally marks to show the players' scores.

Type: Arts and Crafts

Materials needed: poster paper, pencils, tape, string, crayons or markers

Number of players: 1

Make a pictograph to show information about household chores. Draw a pictograph like the one on page 258. Make it about household chores and put the names of people in your house in the pictograph. What picture will you use for your key? A broom? A sponge? Tie a piece of string to a pencil, and tape the other end of the string to the poster paper. Hang this up. Then, draw a picture for each time someone completes a chore.

Has your child breezed through the activities? If so, he or she can work on this Using Your Head activity independently.

Using Your Head

[15] minutes

*Grab some **crayons** and **markers**!*

Scientists are keeping track of the types of animals they see. Find each type of animal and count the number you can see. Then, fill in the bar graph and color the animals in the picture.

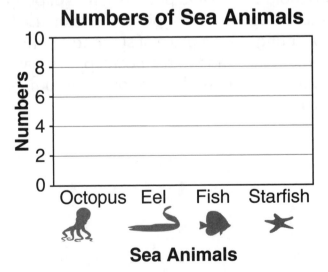

Answers: There are 2 octopi, 6 eels, 4 striped fish, and 8 starfish.

Cracking the Third Grade

Range, Mode, and Mean

We live in a data-driven world filled with information about everything from how many people live in a certain area to who likes what flavor ice cream. We use data to make key decisions: what doctor to choose, what dinner to eat, how much to pay for things, and so on. While data is crucial, sometimes it seems our lives are dominated by data. We wonder what our kids' futures will be—strapping techno-gadgets to their brains, crunching numbers all the time, following streams of flowing data?

You know that your kids need to be comfortable understanding and using data. It's key for their lives today, and it's absolutely crucial for the future that they will be a part of creating.

By thinking about data in terms of range, mode, and mean, your child is starting to practice "viewing" data as a resource. The numbers aren't something to be memorized (there are too many numbers and sets of data in the world to memorize them all!)—the numbers are something to be understood. By having a chance to play around with range, mode, and mean, your kid can get more comfortable looking at data, pondering it, analyzing it, and even developing opinions about it.

First things first: Get a sense of what your kid already knows. Turn the page and tell your kid to Jump Right In!

Here's what you'll need for this lesson:
- *paper*
- *pencils*
- *timer or clock*

Jump Right In!

Tabby and Jacob moved to a new neighborhood. They met their new neighbors and learned a lot about them.

1. Jacob learned how many years each of his neighbors had been living on their street.

   1, 2, 2, 4, 4, 6, 9

   What is the range of this data?

   A. 2

   B. 4

   C. 7

   D. 8

2. Tabby and Jacob learned that some of their neighbors have pets, and some do not. They wrote down how many pets are in each house.

   0, 0, 1, 2, 2, 4, 5

   What is the mean number of pets in each house?

   A. 1

   B. 2

   C. 5

   D. 14

3. Tabby found out the ages of the kids in her new neighborhood.

   5, 6, 7, 8, 9, 9, 12

   She wanted to find out the most common age. What is the mode of this set of data?

   A. 7

   B. 8

   C. 9

   D. 11

A new animal shelter in the neighborhood counted up how many animals were adopted on different days. Use this information to answer the questions below.

Animals Adopted

Day	Number of Animals
Monday	3
Tuesday	2
Wednesday	0
Thursday	5
Friday	5

4. Write the data in order from least to greatest.

_____

5. What is the least number of animals adopted on one day?

_____

What is the greatest number of animals adopted on one day?

_____

What is the range?

_____

6. What is the mean number of animals adopted on one day?

_____

7. What is the mode?

_____

Excellent Job!

 *Checking In*

ⒶAnswers for pages 262 and 263:

1. D
2. B
3. C
4. An A+ answer: 0, 2, 3, 5, 5
5. An A+ answer: 0 animals, 5 animals, 5 animals
6. An A+ answer: 3 animals
7. An A+ answer: 5 animals

Did your child get the correct answers? If so, ask your child to explain the terms *mean*, *median*, and *mode* in his own words.

Did your child get any of the answers wrong? If your child got both questions 1 and 5 incorrect, then she might have difficulty with finding the range. If your child got both questions 2 and 6 incorrect, then she might have difficulty finding the mean (or average). If your child got both questions 3 and 7 incorrect, then she might have difficulty finding the mode. Review the terms and demonstrate applying them with questions 5, 6, and 7. Then, ask your child to work on questions 1, 2, and 3 again.

 *Watch Out!*

Many third graders are unfamiliar with the terms *mean*, *mode*, and *range*. They may have heard the word *mean* as meaning "mean or nasty." They may have heard *range* referring to the stove in their kitchen. To help your child remember, give him this memory tool.

- **Mean** is the **average.** (Your kid can think, "On **average**, I like to say what I **mean**," or think up another helpful sentence.)
- **Mo**de is the thing that happens the **mo**st (both words start with "mo").
- **Range** is the difference between the least and greatest numbers in a set of data. (Your kid can think of "Home, home on the range, where the deer and the antelope play." Tell your kid that the deer and antelope walk from one edge of the range all the way to the other edge of the range. So, to find the range, your kid should order the numbers from least to greatest. Then, your kid should find the number on one edge, then the other edge, and then find the difference.)

What to Know...

Review these skills with your child this way:

- The **range** is the difference between the least and greatest numbers in a set of data.

- The **mode** is the number(s) or item(s) that occurs the most often in a set of data.

- The **mean** is the average of the numbers in a set of data. The mean is calculated by adding the numbers in a set of data and then dividing by the number of items of data.

Your kid might have heard people at football games saying a team was "down by" or "ahead by" a certain number of points. If so, your child heard people talking about range.

Order data from least to greatest: 12, 48.

Subtract the least from the greatest to find the **range.**

48 – 12 = 36

Ask your child to find the range. Check that your child found the range correctly.

Your kid is familiar with mean and mode if he watches swimming, ice skating, gymnastics, dog shows, or reality TV shows. And of course, mean (average) is used all the time with school grades.

Your kid may have watched a reality TV show where contestants sing and are judged.

Music Contest

Add the data together: 7 + 9 + 5 = 21.

Divide by number of items of data to find the **mean.**

21 ÷ 3 = 7

Your kid may have read about the medals won by different teams during the Olympics.

Medals

Teams	Number of Medals
Team A	2
Team B	5
Team C	7
Team D	2

Order data from least to greatest: **2, 2,** 5, 7.

Identify the value that occurs the most often to find the **mode**: 2.

Ask your child to find the mean and the mode. Check that your child found them correctly.

On Your Way to an "A" Activities

Type: Game/Competitive
Materials needed: paper, pencils, a timer or clock
Number of players: 2 or more

Play "How Can That Be?" Each player will pick a number between 1 and 100. This will be your mean. Now, each player has to come up with a set of numbers with that mean. Each player should try to come up with as many sets as possible in 5 minutes. For example, if the mean is 16, a player could write the data sets 1, 31 ($1 + 31 = 32 \div 2 = 16$) and 12, 19, 17 ($12 + 19 + 17 = 48 \div 3 = 16$). When time is up, check each other's work. Each player gets 1 point for each correct set. Then, do the same with mode and range. Whoever has the most points at the end wins.

Type: Active
Materials needed: none
Number of players: 2 or more

Play "In My Head." One player thinks of 2 numbers and says them aloud. The other players work together to find the mean, median, or mode of the data set. Then, these players say the number they found but do NOT say if they found the range, mode, or mean. The first player now has to figure out if it's the range, mode, or mean. For example, if the first player says "1 and 11," the other players could find the range and say "10." Then, the first player has to figure out that this is the range. Once the player has identified this correctly, another player should take a turn saying 2 numbers. Once everyone has had a chance, you can make the game harder by working with 3 numbers!

Has your child breezed through the activities? If so, he or she can work on this Using Your Head activity independently.

Using Your Head

[**10** minutes]

*Grab a **pencil**!*

At a singing contest, the judges lost some of the contestants' scores. Help figure out the missing scores!

1. The first singer got three scores. One is missing. Her average was 8. What is the missing score?

   6, 9, _____

   A. 3

   B. 9

   C. 10

2. The second singer got three scores. One is missing. The range of his scores was 10. What is the missing score?

   2, 7, _____

   A. 3

   B. 5

   C. 12

3. The third singer got three scores. One is missing. The mode was 3. What is the missing score?

   3, 9, _____

   A. 3

   B. 5

   C. 6

Answers: 1. B; 2. C; 3. A

Probability

You and your kid see some clouds outside. Do you take an umbrella? Do you not take one and risk getting wet? Rather than guess, you probably check the weather forecast, which tells you the chance of rain. Every day we rely on probabilities to guide our decisions, big and small (like what to wear). We use probabilities to inform us on a range of things (like the possible results of an election). While right now, your kid doesn't want to hear the predicted results at the end of a voting day, she does need to be able to look at the information given and use it to make decisions.

Right now, your kid probably has experience guessing what's likely to happen or unlikely to happen when playing games. But to develop that skill, she's got to be able to figure out what is *certain, more likely, less likely,* or *impossible* to happen. Then, she's also got to figure out how to express probability in terms of fractions. Because fractions are new to most third graders, your kid will most likely benefit from review and practice.

First things first: Get a sense of what your kid already knows. Turn the page and tell your kid to Jump Right In!

Here's what you'll need for this lesson:
- paper
- pencils
- number cube
- colored paper
- scissors
- glue
- crayons or markers

Judson, May, and Nelly are getting a snack after school. They are picking a snack out of a grocery bag.

1. Judson picks a snack from the bag without looking. What is the chance that he will get a piece of fruit?

   A. certain

   B. more likely

   C. less likely

   D. impossible

2. May picks a snack from the bag without looking. What is the chance that she will get a banana?

   A. $\dfrac{1}{4}$

   B. $\dfrac{1}{5}$

   C. $\dfrac{4}{5}$

   D. $\dfrac{4}{1}$

3. Nelly picks a snack from the bag without looking. What is the chance that she will get an orange?

    A. certain

    B. more likely

    C. less likely

    D. impossible

At the fair, you can turn a spinner in a game to win a prize.

4. What is the probability that a person will win a t-shirt—certain, more likely, less likely, or impossible?

_____

_____

5. Write a fraction to show the probability that a person will win a goldfish.

_____

Excellent Job!

 **Checking In**

Ⓐ Answers for pages 270 and 271:

1. A

2. C

3. D

4. An A+ answer: "The chance of getting a t-shirt is less likely."

5. An A+ answer: "The probability of winning a goldfish is $\frac{3}{6}$, or $\frac{1}{2}$."

Did your child get the correct answers? If so, ask your child to identify what snack the kids would be less likely to get (apple) and what snack they would be more likely to get (banana).

Did your child get any of the answers wrong? If so, go over the terms *certain, more likely, less likely,* and *impossible.* For question 1, it's *certain* that Judson will pick fruit because only fruit is in the bag (there are no options other than fruit). It would be *more likely* for him to pick a banana because there are more bananas than apples. It would be *less likely* for him to pick an apple because there are fewer apples than bananas. It would be *impossible* for him to pick a piece of candy because there is no candy in the bag.

 **Watch Out!**

Did your kid think the probability was the number of times something was shown—instead of the number of times out of the total number of possibilities? For example, with question 5, your kid may have thought the probability of getting a goldfish was 3 because goldfish show up on the spinner 3 times. Remind your kid that the probability is the chance an event could happen out of the total number of possible events. There are 6 equal sections on the spinner, so the chance of getting a goldfish is 3 out of 6, or $\frac{3}{6}$.

Third Graders Are...

You and your kid probably play games all the time. When playing cards, board games, or other games, try to talk about the game in terms of chance. For example, you could talk about the chance of landing on a certain space, rolling a certain number, or getting a certain card. Talking about chance with your kid can help him understand the meaning of probability.

What to Know...

Kids have an intuitive sense of probability from playing games, sharing food, and picking chores.

Review this skill with your child this way:

- **Probability** is the likelihood that an event will happen. You can describe probability using words like *certain, more likely, less likely,* and *impossible.*

Your kid might reach to grab a cookie and randomly pick a cookie from a cookie jar.

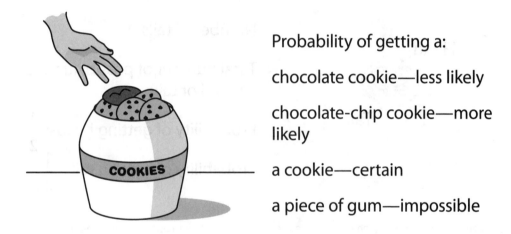

Probability of getting a:

chocolate cookie—less likely

chocolate-chip cookie—more likely

a cookie—certain

a piece of gum—impossible

Ask your child what type of cookie there is more of: chocolate or chocolate chip. Then, explain that because there are more chocolate-chip cookies than chocolate cookies, you are more likely to randomly pick a chocolate-chip cookie. Ask your child why it's impossible to pick a piece of gum from the cookie jar.

Your child can also describe probability using numbers and fractions.

Review this skill with your child this way:

- Probability can be shown as a number from 0 (no chance) to 1 (certain). Often, probability is written as a fraction. The numerator (the top number) is the chance of the event happening, and the denominator (the bottom number) is the number of total possible events.

Your child uses probability when flipping a coin.

Number of heads: 1

Number of tails: 1

Total number of possibilities: 2 (head or tail)

Head
Tail

Probability of getting heads: $\dfrac{1}{2}$

Probability of getting tails: $\dfrac{1}{2}$

Ask your child how many chances there are of getting a head (one) and how many possible results could happen (2—heads or tails). Then, explain how the result that you want is in the numerator and the total number of possible results is in the denominator.

On Your Way to an "A" Activities

20 minutes

Type: Active
Materials needed: number cube (die), paper, colored paper, scissors, glue, crayons and markers, pencils
Number of players: 2 or more

Play "Riddler." With the other players, make prizes using the paper, crayons, markers, glue, and art supplies. Then, one player pretends to be the "Riddler." The Riddler rolls the number cube. Then, the Riddler asks a probability question using the number shown. The first player to correctly answer the question wins a prize. For example, if the Riddler rolls a 4, he could ask, "What is the probability of rolling a 4?" Or if the Riddler rolls a 3, he could ask, "What is the probability of rolling an odd number?"

10 minutes

Type: Game/Competitive
Materials needed: none
Number of players: 2 or more

Play "Chance!" Whenever you hear anyone talking about chance or probability, say "Chance!" Then, if possible, try to figure out the chance using the terms *certain, more likely, less likely,* and *impossible.* The player who says "Chance!" and correctly explains the chance first gets a point. For example, while at the mall, you might hear someone saying, "Almost all the parking spaces were taken!" A player who says "Chance!" could explain that "It's *less likely* to find a parking space because there are fewer open parking spaces than taken parking spaces." The player with the most points wins!

Has your child breezed through the activities? If so, he or she can work on this Using Your Head activity independently.

Using Your Head

[15 minutes]

*Grab a **pencil**!*

At the local fair, there is a game of chance. Figure out how to win the different prizes, and answer the questions.

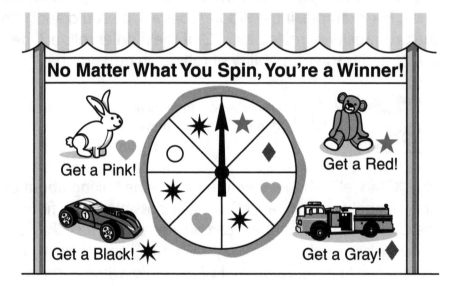

No Matter What You Spin, You're a Winner!

Get a Pink!

Get a Red!

Get a Black!

Get a Gray!

1. What's the probability of winning a bear? _____

2. What's the probability of winning a car? _____

3. The sign says, "No matter what you spin, you're a winner." Is it true that you could always win something with every spin? Why or why not?

_____

Answers: 1. $\frac{3}{8}$; 2. $\frac{1}{8}$; 3. No, because you could land on a white circle, and no prizes are given for this.

Notes

Notes

Notes

Notes

Notes

Notes